Kesava Menon is an analyst and writer on political affairs. He was *The Hindu*'s first Pakistan Correspondent, from July 1990 to October 1993.

Menon started his journalistic career in *Patriot* in the summer of 1984 before switching to *The Hindu* in September that year. He joined as a Staff Reporter in the Delhi Bureau and became Senior Reporter in 1985 and then a Special Correspondent in 1987. He did a lot of ground reporting with the Delhi Bureau, covering the second phase of the Khalistan movement, the beginning of the Kashmir uprising and rural issues in Madhya Pradesh, Haryana and western Uttar Pradesh.

After Pakistan, following a brief stint as an Assistant Editor in *The Hindu*'s Chennai headquarters, he was posted to Bahrain as the paper's West Asia correspondent, covering the whole WANA region from Iran to Morocco and Turkey to Oman from 1994 to 2002. During this period he travelled extensively in the area and reported on several major events and developments. Between 2002 and 2009, he was an Associate Editor with *The Hindu* based in Chennai and responsible for writing editorials on international affairs. He then served as Editor of the Malayalam newspaper *Mathrubhumi* for eight years until his retirement in 2017.

He lives in Kozhikode, Kerala with wife Nandini, daughter Durga and mother Nalini.

Never Tell Them We Are the Same People

NOTES ON PAKISTAN

Kesava Menon

SPEAKING TIGER

SPEAKING TIGER BOOKS LLP
125A, Ground Floor, Shahpur Jat, near Asiad Village,
New Delhi 110049

First published by Speaking Tiger Books 2023

ISBN: 978-93-5447-322-7
eISBN: 978-93-5447-327-2

10 9 8 7 6 5 4 3 2 1

Typeset in Garamond Premier Pro by SÜRYA, New Delhi
Printed at Chaman Enterprises, New Delhi

In memory of my beloved Edathi,
my elder sister Shobhana.
She was a little woman
with a huge big heart.

CONTENTS

INTRODUCTION
Loathing and Curiosity

'They're a ferocious people, aren't they?'

The question was posed by an elderly gentleman in Chennai. I had been posted to the headquarters of *The Hindu* after my stint in Pakistan and was trying to rent accommodation. This prospective landlord, who had evidently been sheltered from the harsher realities of life, was just as obviously revealing an outlook shaped by the decades of vituperation unleashed by opinion makers in each country against the other.

How do you answer such a question without sounding patronizing, insulting or bombastic? An answer did bounce around in the recesses of my brain, that an Indian who had lived among Pakistanis for three years must be fairly formidable himself. Such a response could hardly be voiced when the point was to convince the man that though not a teetotaller or vegetarian, I was a peaceable fellow who did not strew bones around the house. An indecipherable mutter had to suffice for the moment.

Indians perceive of and respond to Pakistanis in all sorts of ways. At the opposite end of the spectrum from my interlocutor in Chennai was the late G.K. Singh, in his time a star of *The Week* magazine. He had come to Pakistan to cover the 1990 parliamentary election along with his photographer Victor George, another great professional who too was to die early and tragically while heroically doing his job. (He was so focused on capturing images at the site of a major landslide that he was taken by surprise when the hill heaved again sending rocks cascading down on him.) Victor was snapping away at a Nawaz Sharif rally when a Muslim League supporter, recognizing him as an Indian, tapped him on the shoulder and told him to go back to his country. A second later, GK tapped the offending Pakistani on his shoulder and told him that they would take him along when they went. Over drinks that evening, I asked GK whether he had not been a bit too reckless. Pat came the reply: 'The Muslim warrior class can never match the Jat Sikhs.'

In attempting to make a generalization about the Indian attitude towards Pakistan, I would have to say that it hovers in the space between the markers set by the above two conversations. I have used the word *markers* instead of *poles* deliberately because sentiment pools so much more densely on the one side than it does on the other. Indians who fear Pakistan are so few in number and the emotion is so dilute even among them that they can hardly be said to exert a pole's magnetic pull. A far, far greater proportion of us look at Pakistan with loathing and contempt, an imbalance that exposes the futility of a policy of terror. If so many atrocities committed over so many years cannot produce anything more than a thin skein of dread among a very limited number of people, one wonders what the effectiveness of such a policy is.

However, that policy has not been abandoned. As it remains, it generates disgust, frustration and fury. Pakistani policy makers seem to have been misled by the presence of an Indian peace camp that was vociferous until recently. They seem to have missed the fact that most peaceniks too are as disgusted with terror tactics as are the bellicose among the Indians. The main difference is that the peace camp does not allow itself to slip into frustration, let alone fury. It is still hopeful of finding a magic formula that will alchemize Pakistan into reasonableness. This hope appears almost as forlorn as Pakistan's dream of bringing India to its knees by resorting to terror. But I will reserve further thoughts on that subject for later.

While intense negativity is the default response that most Indians have towards their country's western neighbour, there does seem to be another emotional current beneath the surface. It is not wistfulness for a happier relationship. A longing for friendship is not very widespread and the subliminal pressure probably has more to do with our need for mental calm. Few Indians want to rid themselves of the deep suspicion they harbour about our neighbour's designs. At the same time, a state of hair-trigger belligerence does become uncomfortable over the long run. These contrary pressures appear to feed a subconscious urge to finely calibrate our outlook towards Pakistan.

This search for the appropriate attitude to be taken in

regard to Pakistan seems implicit in the instinctive query directed at me when I say that I had once lived in that country.

'What is it like?' people ask and the question is always framed in the present tense.

It does not appear to matter to the questioners that I left Pakistan twenty-nine years ago and have never been back. The possibility that the country might have changed apparently does not occur to them. It is perhaps an indication of their belief that Pakistan cannot change; not for the better at any rate.

It is also an acknowledgement of the reality that most of them will never be able to see for themselves. As such the query seems intended to draw out information on an interesting, even important, though not particularly pressing subject. Given this mix of disdain and curiosity, the query actually comes out in the following way even when it does not: 'I don't want to go anywhere near that place but what is it like anyway?'

Irrespective of the relationship they have with their spouses' families, Indians can well empathize with Ian Botham's comment that Pakistan is the place to which a man would like to send his mother-in-law.

Further, the question is invariably phrased in the manner outlined above. The words are always 'What is it like?' even when people on both sides of the exchange know that the real intent is to find out 'what *they* are like'.

Everyone knows that Indians and Pakistanis get along quite well on every bit of real estate outside the subcontinent. Such a twist is perhaps a by-product of the South Asian habit of keeping wardrobes of identities. We know that subcontinental people casually make identity changes depending on the situation, and the true, basic self is revealed only within the confines of the home. So the question that is asked is essentially on these lines—'What are the Pakistanis like when they are in their country?' Or, as we Malayalis would put it—'What are they like when they've changed into their *lungis* and feel free?'

Even when the question is framed like this, the intent is not so much to find out how Pakistanis deal with all issues in their lives. What is sought to be ascertained is the attitude that those people have towards India and Indians when they are in their own country and can show their true feelings. Since the policy that the Islamic Republic has pursued in respect of India has been essentially the same throughout, there does seem to be reason to presume that it has been consistently endorsed by the people. Yet, we also know that Pakistani democracy is far weaker than ours. If ordinary people on our side can influence national policy only to a certain extent, those on the other can do far less. Is it also not possible that the psychological and economic strain wrought by the constant state of belligerence is replicated across the border?

An obvious follow-up question is whether time has not made a difference. Both countries have changed in thirty years and even moderately perceptive Pakistanis know that the equations between them have also been drastically transformed. India's economic take-off, its enhanced global standing and the results of seventy-five years of development effort are recognized. But from the commentaries in the

English press and the electronic media, it is evident that there is as yet no readiness to forego hostility let alone bury the grievances feeding it. As I do not read Urdu, I do not even want to venture into what that customarily intemperate media is spouting these days.

Incidentally, the persistence of the question, whether ordinary Pakistanis subscribe to the policy of hostility towards India as strongly as the makers and implementers of it, also provides a justification for writing a book about my time in that country. If the policy had been dramatically recast, the question would not even arise. Such a transformation would have implied that the social factors sustaining the antagonistic policy had atrophied. And either the masses could have forced the recasting or the rulers confident that the people would go along. In that case, observations about a society made nearly thirty years ago would have lost much of their relevance. Since the policy remains unchanged, the reasonable assumption is that underlying circumstances remain likewise. Material that throws light on those factors will continue to have value.

The durability of the policy also indicates that Pakistani perceptions about India are very deep sunk and a tremendous effort might be needed to uproot them. There is no evidence whatsoever that efforts made towards this end have achieved any success. But this book will be of little worth if it merely confirms what everyone knows. Besides, how well do Indians actually know the writhings of the psyche behind the rock face of hostility? My justification for this book is that no Indian can fathom the complexity of this mindset unless he or she has lived in Pakistan. In living there you feel the ever varying tones of the attitudes your country arouses. When you viscerally know the emotional force directed at you because of your national identity, you are better able to gauge the degree to which it is monolithic or monochromatic.

Several senior Pakistani journalists had urged me to write about my experiences in their country as soon as I had settled back in my own. M.B. Naqvi, one of the most respected among them, repeated the suggestion with some vehemence when I met him years later. I could not do so until now because I was unable to figure out what I should write about. There seemed to be no new angle from which I could approach this topic. Until I thought of good people like A.B.S. Jaffri and Pir Nazakat Shah as well as a few creeps who shall stay nameless for now, and a track seemed to open before me.

This book is not wholly about a recollection of facts that occurred nearly three decades ago or a regurgitation of analyses made at that time. It is more of an effort to record the emotions I felt when dealing with the people and conditions of another country and the reactions I seemed to trigger. That being so, the delay seems appropriate. It has not been so long that memories have faded into soft sepia. Yet, being about emotions, the distancing in time has probably helped the attainment of better balance.

When people want to know what Pakistanis are really like, it is pretty obvious that they are not fully satisfied with the mental picture they have been forming. A host of impressions have pinged on their minds. They still want additional authentication or a fine-tuning of proportions before they embed a conception shaped largely by second-hand information, which is the best they can hope to get.

They have seen the images of wild-eyed mullahs exhorting even wilder-eyed and frothier-mouthed hordes to undertake jihad. They have read of mealy-mouthed politicians in 'Awami *libaas*'—what Indians would generally refer to as the Pathani suit—parroting the rhetoric of the streets before certain audiences and high-minded platitudes before others. They have gone online to hear former test cricketers threatening to send Indian heads flying like cricket balls hit for sixes, and others needlessly bleating aloud their belief in the two-nation theory.

Terrorist strikes that mow down our people certainly have the force to cement negativity. Yet the average Indian does not appear to be completely convinced that he or she has the full picture. The '*aam aadmi*' might not have the time or inclination to work at correcting the image forming in his head but does seem to think that it is somewhat off focus. Questions do lurk somewhere in Indian minds.

While a larger or smaller number of Pakistanis are fanatic or insane, all of them surely cannot be? Aren't there people in that land who have other lives, who are not being shown on the screens? Even some who join the crazies must have other interests that they turn to once the cameras are pointed elsewhere? How did Pakistan otherwise produce so many great hockey, cricket and squash players? Aren't there people across the border who listen to Lata and Kishore as much as they tune in to Nusrat Fateh Ali Khan? How can their best serials match our best movies if everyone is out in the streets clamouring for holy war? They do operate a railway system, they manufacture cars, they run businesses and universities and have armed forces that do not appear incapable! Can they do all this if they spend all their time with their heads buried in the Quran?

Obviously not, and I can cite a whole slew of anecdotes to portray ordinary, day-to-day life in the Islamic Republic. That too can wait. What people want to know, what they want answered when they ask their loaded question is whether there is something unique to the Pakistani psyche that sets them apart from Indians. Or, if you really come down to it, from human beings as we commonly know the species to be.

~

Much the same amorphous mix of questions and prescribed attitudes would rise in my mind before I was given the Pakistan assignment. Perhaps I felt the anger more acutely than many others in the country since I had been covering the second phase of the Khalistan insurrection for about five years and the Kashmiri militancy since its outbreak in April 1989. There was no need for me to read about or listen to newscasts to know about the carnage Pakistan was engineering in our country. Evidence of it was quite often right before my eyes in fields, markets and hospitals.

At that time I had an operational range wide enough to satisfy any journalist. Attached to the Delhi Bureau of *The Hindu* as I was, my beats when in station included the Janata Dal, the Left and often enough the Bharatiya Janata Party as well. That was not all. For a week or more every month, I was on the roads in Punjab, Haryana, Madhya Pradesh and sometimes west Uttar Pradesh reporting for the paper on a daily basis and gathering material for fortnightly *Frontline* articles. The true 'boondocks correspondent' who had not the faintest dream about a foreign posting round the corner!

As in all facets of the India–Pakistan interaction, media coverage of one country by outfits headquartered in the other had its own peculiar pattern. Indian newspapers (there were no private TV channels at that time and the internet was no more than an embryo in some geek's brain) could not just obtain visas and open offices in Pakistan. Or the other way round. Through some tedious process the two governments had come to an agreement that each would allow three media outlets from the other to operate within its territory.

For a few years Press Trust of India, All India Radio/Doordarshan and *Times of India* provided our contingent in Islamabad while Associated Press of Pakistan, *Jang* and Radio Pakistan/Pakistan TV did the needful from New Delhi. Then, after another bout of negotiations, the two governments decided to allow one more outlet each with *The Hindu* and *Dawn* (of Karachi), as front-runners. *Dawn* backed out a little while later, throwing *The Hindu*'s chances into jeopardy. Then one of those rare flashes of sanity that illuminate the bilateral exchange burst into the noonday sky and the Pakistanis told *The Hindu* that it could come anyway.

Within the bureau, my dear friend and mentor Appan Menon was the obvious choice and he began processing his papers. At that time *The Hindu*'s investigation into what the paper termed l'affaire Bofors was well underway. With parliamentary elections due in a few months, pressure began to build on the paper from outside. That had repercussions for the cohesiveness of the management and staff. There was no direct impact on the journalists in Delhi or elsewhere though the general atmosphere definitely became less pleasant than what we were accustomed to.

At about the same time, Prannoy Roy was putting together the programme 'The World This Week', the fledgling venture that would eventually grow into NDTV. He wanted Appan as the presenter. This 'pull' factor was, I think, far more critical than the 'push' generated by the turbulence afflicting the paper and Appan left in late 1989 or early '90. To my utter surprise, G. Kasturi, Editor and everything else in The Hindu Group, chose me as the replacement. N. Ram also pushed me to 'go for it'.

All of a sudden I became supernumerary to the bureau. There was little point in keeping me on the beats when I would be leaving in a few weeks, was the general idea. Turf battles are never easy to forego and I did get some nasty pleasure in doing what exclusives I could before the new guys took over. That time would have been better spent in preparing for my next assignment. While some work was put in to that end, greater maturity or common sense could have led me to cogitate more on my approach to Pakistan.

Any Indian trying to get a grip on the condition of the subcontinent has to confront the reality of Partition. Our conceptualizations of how we came to be as we are can begin with the contemplation of the Indus Valley Civilization or even further back to the first and second waves out of Africa. But Partition and Independence will always mark a watershed because the nation-states of today came into being in the lands bordered by the Himalayas and the Indian Ocean in 1947. As far as I am concerned, the division of the land is not a matter that arouses much passion.

As everyone knows, those of us who live south of the Satpuras did not suffer the massacres of the founding year. A desire to avenge co-religionists is not absent among South Indians but it was very uncommon during my formative years. Although mine is an extremely devout family—steeped in all three streams, Vaishnava, Shaiva and Shakta—I do not remember ever hearing any relatives or associates talking let alone raving about the Muslim marauders of Partition times. As far as the generation preceding mine was concerned, North Indian Hindus were an unfamiliar species, so where would Pathans or Punjabi Mussalmans figure in?

Perhaps we Malabaris did not get worked up about Partition because we had our own history of communal conflict. My great grandfather had been one of the main leaders of the Non-Cooperation/Khilafat Movement in Malabar; had been unable to stop its deterioration into the Moplah uprising of 1921 despite heroic last-minute efforts to broker peace; and had done much to heal the wounds thereafter. The anti-Hindu aspect of that violent outbreak was very much part of the caste memory during my childhood.

However, 1921 did not mark the definitive tipping point in our historical consciousness because the same pattern had unfolded before. Communal co-existence had been first disturbed during the century-long struggle against the Portuguese when the Samuthiris of Kozhikode (Zamorins of Calicut) had a falling out with their fighting ship captains the Kunjali Marakkars. Hindu–Muslim strife had flared ferociously between 1761 and 1792 when the Mysoreans under Hyder Ali and Tipu Sultan had tried to impose their will on Malabar and run into resistance. In the British period, beginning 1805 or thereabouts, Hindus cooperated wholeheartedly with the authorities in brutally putting down the Muslim revolts, which usually began with some act of horror. All these phases were also marked by tales of communal cooperation, very often against co-religionists.

Warfare in the *dehat* is not for the squeamish. By the time the advent of democracy ushered in new ways of settling disputes, weariness with the brutalities of the past seems to have weighed in as shackles on both communities. As I was growing up, I was made aware of inter-communal friendships though I was also conditioned to a subliminal wariness. My lack of fear of the Muslim bogeyman was also probably attributable to the fact that my caste men had re-cemented their position as the hegemons of Malabar a half-dozen generations or more before I was born.

For this reason, I have never been burdened by the 'trauma of subordination'. I can track the historical argument that causes sections of Hindus in the Gangetic plain, especially the natives of the one-time administrative-centres of successive Sultanates, to be so burdened. But I simply cannot feel the emotion myself. This is the point at which advocates of Hindutva lose me completely. Whenever pressured to feel victimized, something deep in me says, 'My ancestors were not lambs and neither am I.'

Lack of emotional baggage of this type was one matter. There were still a lot of preconceptions instilled in the brain by virtue of being an Indian with a default antagonism towards Pakistan. Corrections had to be made while ensuring that I did not become overly sympathetic to a nasty neighbour. From the forays into the boondocks I had learnt something about the temptation to slip into a variant of the Stockholm Syndrome. Much mental clarity was provided by two former foreign secretaries, S.K. Singh and K.P.S. Menon, and two senior journalists, Rajendra Sareen of POT (Public Opinion Trends) and K.K. Katyal of my own paper, who very kindly found time to brief me. To my mind, the cleverest question I asked them was whether the Pakistanis actually had a sense of themselves as a people. They all, none of them dovish by any means, answered unequivocally in the affirmative.

Questions of this fundamental nature had to be set aside for a while as there was so much going on within the Islamic Republic when I landed in Lahore in late July 1990, missed the connecting flight and completed my journey the next day by flying coach. (These were vans or mini-buses that carried about twenty passengers apiece faster and with greater comfort than either regular buses or trains.) As has often been the case in that country's turbulent history, Pakistan seemed to be hovering on the edge of disaster. That was the impression given by the facts as well as the lamentations in the media. A good deal of this churning was outside the Indian experience.

Pakistan had started its third experiment with democracy a few years before but the dispensation had not gained much sustenance. Zia-ul-Haq's grim shadow loomed over the whole country even though he had died in 1988. Other than the diehard Jiyalas (loyalists of the Pakistan Peoples

Party), few believed that the incumbent Prime Minister Benazir Bhutto would gather to herself the might ascribed to the only real democratic leaders in the country's history—the Mohammed Ali Jinnah–Liaquat Ali Khan combine of the first experimental phase and her own father Zulfiqar Ali Bhutto of the second from December 1971 to his ouster in July 1977.

Trouble had been brewing for Benazir from the beginning of her tenure two years earlier and was fast coming to a head. Nawaz Sharif, then chief minister of Punjab and also a henchman of the establishment at the time, was leading a political insurrection against the federal government. Her 'uncles', acolytes of her father who had clout in their own right, were believed to have grown restive and seemed ready to bolt from her camp. General Mirza Aslam Beg, the Chief of Army Staff seemed a less malevolent figure than Zia but he was hand-in-glove with President Ghulam Ishaq Khan who was the very embodiment of the establishment's loathing for democracy and democrats.

Benazir was ousted from office about a week after I took up my assignment. Ghulam Mustafa Jatoi, one of the 'uncles', now no longer part of the PPP, was appointed caretaker prime minister and an election was scheduled for later that year. From the outset of the campaign, there could be little doubt that all was being done to ensure the victory of Sharif and his Islami Jamhoori Ittehad ('Islamic Democratic Alliance')—comprised mainly of the Muslim League, the Jamaat-e-Islami and some religious parties. The IJI won a comfortable majority; the PPP was reduced almost to the level of a Sindh-based outfit, and the establishment was back as the real power behind the elected cabinet.

This jury-rigged, largely anti-people, ruling system controlled the destiny of a country where civil society had been virtually decimated. The press was bravely waging its guerrilla campaign to get at the truth but there were no institutions to take up issues it exposed. Trade unions and professional associations functioned in supplicatory fashion, concerned with their narrow demands. There were few non-governmental organizations, of which barely a couple or so were concerned with rights issues and these were completely ignored by the powers of the land.

Politicians were so caught up in issues pertaining to their nests, particularly about how to feather them, that they had no time for the concerted effort needed to draw inviolable lines. Were it not for the fear of contempt proceedings, commentaries on the judiciary's functioning and pronouncements could well have been abusive. There were no institutions that were interested in improving their own methods and setting benchmarks for others to follow. A concept of working dispassionately towards an ideal had not crystallized though the yearning for it was palpable in quite a bit of the writing in the press.

Despotism's brutalities had quelled nationalist fervour in the smaller provinces. Insurgencies directed at gaining independence had been abandoned at least temporarily in Balochistan, Sindh and the North West Frontier Province (which was to be renamed Khyber Pakhtunkhwa more than a decade later). That had not brought peace to these parts. Freedom fighters had turned into ethnic warriors who waged bloody struggles against migrants from other areas.

The backlash of the war against the Soviets in Afghanistan

was being felt in many parts of the country. Heroin and Kalashnikovs had apparently flooded the market to go by the reports of seizures of one item and the frequent use of the other. Jihadi factories in the Frontier, Pak-Occupied Kashmir, Muridke and other sites had already activated their production lines and the day was not far off when the whole lot would begin cannibalizing their country. A start on the downslide was already evident with Barelvis and Deobandis squaring off against each other and both itching to attack the Shias.

Although pre-occupied with domestic and neighbourhood issues, Pakistan could not ignore developments elsewhere in the world. Iraq's invasion of Kuwait almost coincided with my arrival in Islamabad. For Pakistan's rulers, the position they needed to take was clear-cut to begin with. Their country's and their countrymen's dependence on the emirates of the Gulf was so pronounced that they readily backed Saudi Arabia. As war loomed ever closer, however, this policy became problematic. The masses, even when not whipped on by the mullahs, were strongly in favour of Saddam Hussein and against the new Crusaders.

Other conflicts involving Muslim communities elsewhere in the world kept disquiet simmering in the streets. Israel's actions against Lebanon and the Palestinians were a constant source of bitterness. The implication of this distant conflict were brought closer home since the United States, the Zionist country's main benefactor, was beginning to be accused once again of betraying Pakistan. With the withdrawal of the Soviets, Washington seemed increasingly disinclined to treat Pakistan as a frontline ally and the barely clandestine nuclear programme was becoming a new irritant in the relationship. In the fevered imagination of those orchestrating street demonstrations, the 'Yehud' (Jews), 'Hanood' (Hindus) and 'Nazara' (Christians) had formed an unholy alliance.

Amidst all this, another Pakistan struggled to survive. This was the society of Bulleh Shah and other Sufi mystic saints; of Amir Khusro, Ghalib and Faiz Ahmad Faiz; of people who honoured Hindu philanthropists for establishing most of the private hospitals and colleges in the country, who could admire Viv Richards and Sunil Gavaskar for their cricketing skills; of the mix of flamboyant Punjabi generosity and Persian *andaaz* that Lahore tried to epitomize; of the Memons and Bohras of Karachi who seemed to act as if Partition had never happened. These traits made for the best of Pakistan and the essence of the goodness seemed to be a gentler, family-centric religiosity.

Also, the whole edifice of the nation was holding together against the odds. With my experience in Pakistan and years of cogitating about it afterwards, the only explanation I have for this mystery is that there were enough people in the country who willingly did their allotted tasks. There were people who cared enough for their fellow citizens or the dignity of their country or their own self-respect to try and do what was needed. That is the essence of the nation's strength. Unfortunately, whatever makes for real value was mostly buried under the piles of nonsense that went on.

After settling down in Islamabad, however, I began to wonder whether those who had asserted that there was something called Pakistaniyat had taken me for a ride. This suspicion arose because India loomed so prominently in the

Pakistani public discourse that their definition of themselves seemed encapsulated in the words: 'We are not those rascals'.

To get a measure of the depths of this obsession it would be useful to turn once again to matters of cricket. We are deeply, even agonisingly, disappointed when we lose to Pakistan but move on the next day with our moods restored to the states they were in before the match. When we win, we are as deeply satisfied that we 'have shown those buggers their place'. Pakistani reactions are on another scale altogether. Defeat is treated as a negation of the nation's existence while victory becomes a euphoric vindicator of all sins. It is like their drinking.

Our diplomatic and journalistic veterans had not misled me. There is a Pakistani soul somewhere, but to get even an idea of its shape takes some doing. The India obsession itself seems to suggest that there is a deep uncertainty about the core of their own nationhood, which in turn causes much intellectual and cultural dissonance. That this sort of psychobabble had sunk deeply into my own mind came out in an incident when I ran into a Pakistani friend in Casablanca a couple of years after I had departed from Islamabad.

It was some silly argument that got a bit heated and brought out the usual 'You Indians', 'You Pakistanis' epithet-throwing equivalent of thumbing our noses at each other. It ended with me saying, 'If a person has an inferiority complex it can be cured, but what do you do when a whole country has one?'

Although my friend produced a scornful sniff in response, I thought I had clinched the argument at that time. But even then I felt that I had not accurately pinpointed the problem. Have I got any closer to the answer after twenty-odd years of cogitating over it? Can a prolonged identity crisis serve as an adequate explanation for this obsessive need to compare themselves with some other? Or, to get the sequencing right, does the obsession stem from a crisis of identity?

After all, we Indians too are currently caught up in a struggle to define ourselves but do not succumb to the temptation of using some other country as the foil. Some forces in our country do have an absurd urge to do that. Hopefully, they will learn from Pakistan's experience that the adoption of such a worldview will only lead to collective neurosis.

~

In getting down to seriously addressing the matter as I write this book, it comes to my mind that until now I might not have unknotted two separate cultural processes working towards the development of a Pakistani narrative, and therefore identity. One is a peoples' attempt to arrive at self-realization by drawing on their history, their capabilities and their hopes for the future. This is a struggle common to all countries, especially those still shedding the vestiges of colonialism. The second strand, which is peculiar to Pakistan, is the pressure applied by organs of the state to compress a natural process into a preset mould. These two strings of the social processes remained intertwined in my mind probably because the official version was promoted so vigorously that the natural process was stifled and made invisible.

All countries, including the most democratic, have official narratives of their evolution that are used as an explanation of their respective presents. Usually, the state adopts this narrative even when it is not the instigator and other institutions then go along. For instance, the National Movement was India's narrative until the turn of the millennium. This was largely an Indian National Congress-inspired story that the official machinery took on board. Currently, as we know, the ruling party at the Centre and its ideological mentor are making a determined effort to drastically reframe this storyline. Large sections of officialdom, academia, media and the chatterati have thrown their weight behind this endeavour.

Countries where democracy has taken root do not follow linear paths when it comes to the shaping of the national narrative. So long as the spirit of dissent is alive, the official line will be challenged. It might not even be dissent but a commitment to independent enquiry that undermines the sponsored narrative and recasts it in unexpected ways. We do not know how the ideological struggle currently broiling India will pan out but we do know that people of diametrically opposite views are vigorously engaged in it; that one version has not attained hegemony despite wielding enormous clout.

Consider the approach to the comprehension of our history between 1200 and 1700 CE. The dominant theme is that of Muslim invasions across the north-western borders of the subcontinent and Hindu resistance. That is certainly the most common conceptualization of the period. However, serious historians have gone beyond this bare-boned template. They have presented solid proof in support of a far more subtle or nuanced version.

Successive batches of scholars at some of our best universities have absorbed these lessons and added their variations. These alternative versions are out in the public domain. Fairly large numbers of people are aware that the story is not so simple. So much so that the argumentation goes on beyond the parameters a powerful set of interests would like to confine it within. India's understanding of itself is enriched in the process. If we are lucky, we may even end up as a more mature nation.

Pakistan's misfortune is that the official storyline has never been seriously and publicly challenged. Although democratic forces under Zulfiqar Ali Bhutto at first and then Nawaz Sharif tried hard to wrest power from the sponsors of this narrative, they did little to correct the storyline itself. Serious counters to the official version have been buried in the shelves reserved for academic dissertations. Solid works produced in the field of history and political economy are smothered under the thick cloud of flatulence that monopolizes space in the public discourse.

Seventy-five years of autocracy, open and hidden, have done that. The term 'Pakistan's permanent establishment' has been around forever and I am as guilty as the next Indian journalist or scholar of having used it as a different way of saying 'You know who I mean!' Facetiousness aside, how do you get away from the reality that the military has always been in control?

I can hear the groans about this book being another repetition of the same old theme. That cannot be helped.

A description cannot change when the reality remains the same. Pakistan cannot be understood if the centrality of the authoritarian element is overlooked.

By the way, the term 'authoritarian' does not encompass only the power that is applied. It should also cover the thinking behind the exercise of that power. Those who wield the power appear convinced that they are the 'authorities' on all subjects under the sun—that they alone have the knowledge or the wisdom to be the final arbiters on all matters.

The term 'establishment' might also be somewhat misleading. It suggests an engineered structure with the armed forces at the base and a series of layers—bureaucracy, feudals, industrialists and mullahs—staggered above. There is reason to think that the phenomenon might be more organic with the military at the core and each and every other element feeding into and off it. Other elements of the organism know where the power lies, have taken what they think is the smart option and grown comfortable with their roles and function in the overall set up.

Feudal landlords have always been prominent in Pakistani politics—the Hayats, Noons and Tiwanas might have been supplanted by others of less renown though with comparably large estates in Punjab but the Bhuttos, Zardaris and other old names still dominate rural Sindh. Large landholders are not absent from the political scene of Balochistan and Khyber Pakhtunkhwa either.

Sajjada Nashins (heads of famous shrines such as the Pirs of Pagaro) combine in themselves spiritual authority, feudal weight and electoral clout. They share this tri-junctional space with heads of religious parties of whom Maulana Fazal-ur-Rehman of the Jamiat Ulema-e-Islam is the most prominent though not the sole representative.

Business magnates from Karachi were joined in the consultative machinery for decision making by their counterparts from Punjab. Of these the Sharifs of the Ittefaq Group became the foremost. The entire asset-owning hierarchy is threaded through and through by offshoots of the military. Officers retire to farmland granted as perks of office; acquire house plots at highly subsidized rates and sell these for huge profit; or set up their children in lucrative businesses. This process was institutionalized through the Fauji (Army), Shaheen (Air Force) and Bahriya (Navy) foundations that were ostensibly set up for the welfare of ex-servicemen but also provided post-retirement sinecures. These foundations run enterprises from bakeries to cement factories.

Relationships between these diverse elements were never purely transactional or business related. Quite often they were supplemented by bonds of matrimony. This pattern continues with perhaps the prime example being Nawaz Sharif's daughter, Maryam Nawaz, and her husband who is a martial Awan and an ex-officer. It is all quite different from the situation in India where Ambanis/Adanis stick to business, Gandhis/Karunanidhis stick to politics and generals retire to their clubs and golf courses. Of course, there is a bit of cross-fertilization here as well but not on the rampant scale at which it goes on in Pakistan.

While other sections of society have found ways to tap into this power system, there can be little doubt that the military and its junior partner the civilian bureaucracy provides it with form and governs its functioning. By virtue of education and professional training, the officer tier, military and civilian, could be said to form a separate class. Their worldview probably derives much from the ethos of the rural landed classes but also appears to be overlaid with a mandarinate's assumption of moral superiority—or, at least, the belief that they are the only true patriots.

I am not directly acquainted with a single Pakistani military man but I suspect that members of this class are better educated than most of their compatriots. To go by the choices available in second-hand book stores in Rawalpindi, which are remarkably eclectic, the military allows itself a mental breadth and depth that it denies to the rest of the country. (I knew this because the names of previous owners written on the fly-leaves of second-hand books often included their ranks.)

Do they see themselves as Janissaries or Mamelukes, the elite warrior classes of once-powerful sultanates that were allowed an expansiveness of mind as an exclusive privilege? Whether they do or not there are enough other signs to conclude that for the 'Khakis' the sponsored national narrative is both a raison d'être and a high-utility tool for obtaining sustenance. They need to keep the minds of their people wrapped in distorted conceptualizations.

To say that the Pakistani military strives to control the national mind is not merely an analytical postulate. Efforts made for this purpose flow from the right, duty and status the Fauj claims for itself. I do not know when the term was coined but the military appears to have finally entered a comfort zone when it started calling itself the 'Guardians of the Pakistan Ideology'.

Still, the groaners referred to above do have a point. Why repeat stuff written before? A couple or three justifications come to mind. Firstly, it is always fun to poke holes in silly stories. Secondly, and more importantly, in the process of recounting my experiences I might just be able to offer insights into how the Pakistani common man deals with the pressures of indoctrination. Thirdly, it is fascinating to watch when the consciousness gets expanded by wider experience and sheer common sense. Such a process is usually cyclical with positive changes rapidly giving way to the negative before the current veers the other way again. For the observer, the fascination is sustained by the possibility that dissent might attain critical mass at some point in time.

Perhaps all the reasons basically boil down to a single one. That the story of the common man's response to this persistent effort at moulding mindsets might not have got enough attention. It might have been presented before but reiterations are necessary because positives must be always encouraged.

When commenting on Pakistan, it is always useful to fix on the establishment's machinations since this approach helps give structure to the presentation. Such a fixation is warranted because the establishment's actions usually provide the rough drafts of explanation for events or phenomena. However, there is a drawback to this approach as it does not take account of the common man's response to the moves made by the powers that be. These responses do not always run along prescribed lines and the flashes of partial or complete defiance throw light on other possibilities. Even a collection of reminiscences that takes note of acts of subversion as well as surrender can surely aid in the understanding of Pakistan.

Some of the incidents to be described bring out the methods by which the tentacles of the ideology are splayed across the national mind. Other episodes bring out the ways in which the intended victims of the octopus dodge the grip. It is a form of guerrilla warfare fought with words, indifference and wit. Those who participate in this insurgency might be doing so more intuitively than consciously. For all that, it is an ongoing effort to snatch, preserve and expand the space for intellectual and cultural emancipation.

This account could have been richer had I been allowed the freedom to travel more widely through the country. Both the Indian and Pakistani governments imposed tight visa regimes and I should actually be grateful that I was given more leeway than my successors, contemporaries or those who preceded. Although journalists were not granted diplomatic immunity, Pakistani officialdom did to an extent grant the courtesies with which governments usually treat the media. Confined to Islamabad-Rawalpindi for most of the time, with a certain degree of flexibility to go to the two entry/exit points—Lahore and Karachi—my wife and I managed at least two memorable outings. Swat and Moenjodaro provided some compensation for the irksome restrictions.

A Boar Before Breakfast

Nandini, my wife, always knew when Pir Nazakat Shah was on the other end of the telephone line even before I had uttered a word. According to her, the giveaway was the beatific smile I would have on my face. Or more accurately, the glazed, happy expression that was the best my features could manage in trying to convey benevolent feelings. Pir Saab was my landlord in Islamabad from 1990 to '93 and our friendship remains as one of the better memories of my three-year stay in Pakistan.

He usually called early in the mornings. The '*salaam alaikums*', '*kaise hains*' and '*khairiyats*' would shoot out before my brain cells were done clicking through the voice-recognition process, shuffling through memory cards, forming a picture of the face at the other end of the line and brought up the last update on our exchanges. The opening phase would last for a while as he enquired about the health of my family and friends and sought assurance that any niggling problems we might have spoken of earlier were under control. It would be my turn then and I would have to go on a bit longer since he had a big family, large landholdings, other properties leased out on rent and also some cattle. (They do rear cows, not just eat the animals.) These exchanges would be liberally interspersed with '*Khuda ki meherbani hai*', '*Allah ta'ala ka shukr hai*' and other salutations to the ultimate benefactor that he would deliver with utter sincerity. He had the hoarse voice of a heavy smoker and he would be a little wheezy by the end of our conversations.

One winter morning in 1992, he drove up to my house without bothering to call beforehand as was his usual practice. He parked a little past my gate, hauled his burly body out from the front seat of his Pajero and proceeded to act in a manner that only added to my perplexity. He had never been anything less than punctilious in observing the boundaries of my domesticity, always coming into my house in the manner of a guest, foregoing the trappings of the owner. This time he flung the gate wide open after a perfunctory greeting and waved in a pickup that had drawn up behind him. The vehicle backed into my driveway, two men hopped out of the cabin and pulled away a tarpaulin that covered the bed of the truck.

Stretched out on the bed was the body of a young wild boar.

~

'*Khet mein maara aaj subah. Aap khaate hain na?*' (We shot it this morning in our field. You eat it, don't you?) Pleasure and concern seemed to be mingled in equal measure in Pir Saab's voice.

The pleasure was of course occasioned by the chance

to offer a gift. The reason for his concern was equally understandable. In all his life, he had probably never offered the flesh of an 'unclean animal' to another person and was worried that the unbeliever before him might consider the gift an insult.

People from the neighbouring district of Hazara, which began on the reverse slope of the Margalla Hills looming behind the Pir as he stood before the gate, might have set his mind at ease. They could have told him that as a Malabari I followed my own dietary rules. But he and his companions were all men of Potohar, more prone to taking employment in the police and the armed forces of the Emirates, quite unlike the Hazaras who toiled alongside Keralites in the construction sites of the Saudi peninsula.

The boar was offloaded in my backyard and the Pir and his companions departed. That left me with the problem of finding a way to skin, gut and carve the game and get rid of the remains. A request for help to the staff of the Indian High Commission was ruled out for a variety of reasons. That left the Sri Lankans, Russians and Chinese. Each of those groups, according to the gossip, had its own way of hunting the hordes of wild boar that thrived in the scrub jungle of the Margallas. The Chinese were quite accessible since their journalists lived in a commune of sorts in the house they had rented together. But the equations between the Indians and the Chinese living in Pakistan were too complicated for this option to be treated as anything more than a last resort.

As on so many matters before the collapse of the Soviet Union, the Russians could be relied upon to help the Indian on the question of the boar as well. This was the period when the Najibullah regime was still clinging to power in Kabul and its sustenance was a common objective for New Delhi and Moscow. If Islamabad-Rawalpindi was the epicentre of the multinational coalition's efforts to topple Najibullah, it was also an important outpost for the few governments struggling to keep the regime in place. Personnel of the two embassies got along famously and there was every hope of friendly assistance from this quarter.

More to the point, the Russians apparently had the most effective system for getting the boars. It was said that their effort to get a roast suckling pig onto the dinner table involved buying heavy calibre cartridges from the black market, rigging a firing mechanism to each bullet and tying the contraption to bushes along the boar trails. Unfortunately for me, on that particular day, every Russian I knew was out of town.

So my thoughts turned to the Lankans. In Arjuna Ranawana, then representing *Asiaweek*, I had a good friend and potential collaborator. Foodwise, Lankans and Malayalis have much in common. Not only do we eat the same rice-based dishes that are called hoppers on the island and *appam* around the backwaters, we also have the same lack of inhibition about what we ingest. There was a small hitch in approaching the Lankans that had to do with diplomatic crosscurrents of the subcontinent. It hadn't been long since the end of the Indian Peace Keeping Force operations, and Sri Lanka's relations with the 'big brother' were not free of strain. Those born in the 1990s and later might not know that India had sent a strong body of troops to Sri Lanka to aid the island's government in controlling the Liberation

Tigers of Tamil Eelam (LTTE). This well-intentioned move turned messy after the Sinhala authorities came to a secret understanding with the LTTE and the Indian army found itself caught in the middle. Pakistan had been wooing the island nation but it sometimes acted as if muscle displays were an indispensable part of its courtship. In this situation, it was often not easy to predict which way the Lankans would jump.

As it turned out, I need not have worried. No one from the Lankan diplomatic mission or from the several, small military liaison teams was available for the boar-butchering exercise. It was strictly to be a journalistic affair. Arjuna, joining me in the hunt for a butcher, suggested that we scout the small colony of Scheduled Castes. Most were Christians and had no misgivings about touching pork. We duly found a cobbler who agreed to do the job once a caveat had been entered and circumvented. He did not know how to cut up and eviscerate a pig though he could do the needful if it was a goat. No problem, we told him, think of it as a goat and gut it as you like!

There was a lot of meat. Bucketsful of it. Even after we had distributed kilos of the stuff among Indians and Lankans, there was enough left to pickle in two or three jars. I wrapped the head, skin and unwanted body parts in plastic and a jute sack, loaded it in the trunk of my car and threw it away in the recesses of the Margallas. That was the end of the story, or should have been but for two small appendices.

The first concerned the butcher. After paying for his services, I asked him whether he did not want some of the meat. He certainly did not, he said, since he was a Muslim.

Religious taboos could apparently be bent though not broken, at least in his case. Such distinctions did not bother our maid Zohra. She was a Pakhtun from the far reaches of the Kurram Agency, and no one had taught her about the religious ban on eating the flesh of animals with cloven hooves that do not chew the cud. She had probably not been taught much more than the Shahada, the declaration of faith. Nandini was finally able to convince Zohra that the meat was forbidden to her. She was a sweet-natured woman but I do not think she ever forgave us for keeping a rich haul away from her great brood of children. (For those confounded by the use of the word 'Agency' in Pakistani administrative nomenclature, here's a quick history lesson: in the heyday of imperialism, the British had placed the wilder parts of the NWFP under officers called Agents; this arrangement continued almost till this millennium.)

It has been more than a quarter century since that day and I sometimes wonder whether the Pakistanis ever got around their boar problem. Although I never came across any news stories or even gossip about those cantankerous beasts ever attacking people, they were a menace. On a couple of occasions, coming back late from parties, our headlights caught great brutes trotting out of and back into the nullah that ran on the other side of the house next to ours. More frequently, we would be warned by fellow trekkers on the splendid trails through the Margallas to turn back as there were boars around. Come to think of it, the story about Russian hunting methods was probably apocryphal. Given the proximity between man and beast, how could the 'Russkies' have planted their trigger-equipped cartridges with the certainty that no humans would be injured?

That particular breed of pork was really succulent probably because the animals in those parts raid the maize fields. With so much prey for the taking, there should have been some panthers around since those supremely cunning predators can survive where few other cats can. However, I do not remember hearing about any panthers or wild cats or any other felines for that matter.

About the only other game that I came across were the ubiquitous quail sold in the Jumma Bazaar and two huge porcupines scuttling down the long driveway from the Prime Minister's house. A friend and I were returning after a fairly pleasant press meet and the sight of those bristling backsides finally scurrying into the undergrowth on one side served to keep the mood going.

~

The real jungle is no longer part of the common experience of Indians as it once was. The denudation is worse west of the border. As far as the dry deciduous and alpine variety are concerned, Pakistan has its stretches. It is still strange to think of a subcontinental country without real wildlife. There must be ibex and probably snow leopards and bears as well in the high mountains and the lands bordering on Kutch might have some wild asses, though Indians might never get to see them. Were the plains of Punjab and Sindh always free of lions when parts of the terrain are not very different from the Gir? Where did Bairam Khan kill the tiger? To a person for whom trips to Thekaddy, Mudumalai, Bandipur, Bandhavgarh and Kaziranga were interwoven into his development, a country without really wild spaces seemed sadly bereft.

Houbara bustards do not look very impressive in pictures but they are apparently much prized as game-birds by falconers. Arab sheikhs had set off quite a furore in the 1980s when they brought large parties to hunt this avian prey in the deserts of Rajasthan and Sindh. I have not seen falconers in action (the fantastic show put up with Brahmani kites in Singapore's Jurong Bird Park is not quite the same thing) and always wondered about the mystique surrounding them. Until I got onto a flight from Bahrain to Qatar and saw the last row left of the aisle occupied by a strange set of passengers. A rather fierce looking Arab was in the aisle seat and on the next he had plonked an elaborate stand on which was perched a definitely ferocious looking bird. Although clamps were fixed on its beak and talons, one look was enough to understand why the third seat had been left empty.

Houbara hunting ceased to be an issue in India soon after the news broke. If I remember right, the official claim was that the hunters had kept their intentions hidden and had been stopped as soon as the facts came into the open. Perhaps that was true or perhaps the falconers were persuaded to go about their pleasures in remoter corners of the Thar. That appeared to have been the case in Pakistan because stray reports of Arabs being sighted near Rahim Yar Khan or Tharparkar or wherever popped up in the press from time to time.

Birds (maybe rabbits as well) were hunted in other parts of the country. On drives out of Islamabad it was not uncommon to see small groups of men with a rifle or shotgun and several sticks trudging through the dry, shallow ravines of the Potohar. Ayaz Amir, columnist with *Dawn* at that time and a parliamentarian later, had once written a nice piece about a *shikar* he had been on near his village in Chakwal.

In other components generally regarded as the benchmarks of a country's natural beauty, Pakistan did not seem too badly off in those days. Or not as badly off as it could have been given the compelling evidence of man's destructive hand. On flights from Karachi to Islamabad, green stretches could be viewed when the neck was craned to take in whatever there was to see before the plane gained altitude. I was never able to determine whether those green patches were forest or orchard.

My first trip into interior Sindh, if it could be called so, was to Thatta. This town and its hinterland were too close to Karachi and not so distant from the Arabian Sea as to qualify as the true interior. The second and last was to see Moenjodaro, and these ancient ruins are so close to Larkana airport that the short coach ride can hardly be described as a venture into the boondocks.

Pakistani tele-serials, which were (arguably still are) better than ours, tended to depict the Sindhi heartland as wild country. In *Chand Grehan*, Jehaniya Shah, villain or rebel depending on the point of view, was shown to be sheltering with a dacoit band in what was described as the 'jungle'. Since the pertinent screenshots showed only thin clumps of dry scrub, it was impossible to imagine that there was more to it. Perhaps there wasn't, except for margins along the shores of the Indus. To the naked eye, the land seemed hard, unyielding and scrub seemed to be about all that it could support.

Years later, in a YouTube interview, I heard Asif Ali Zardari wax eloquent about the richness of the soil in his home province of Sindh and in Balochistan. It produced good, long staple cotton and would yield greater bounties if irrigated more extensively; Benazir's husband surely knew what he was talking about.

The central plain of Punjab was certainly more lush. Crisscrossed by canals as it was, it gave the same sense of richness as the plains of Malwa, Doaba and Majha on our side of the border. Somehow, I never got to visit these parts during the monsoon (it probably coincided with my periods of leave), so the Ravi near Lahore was never more than a not-too-wide, not-too-deep stream to my eyes. The Sutlej was too south of the paths I travelled on, though she must have appeared much like her sister. Part of the explanation is that the operationalizing of the Indus Waters Treaty could not have left much for the downstream except in the rainy season. Signed in Karachi in 1960 by Jawaharlal Nehru and Ayub Khan, the Treaty was a settlement for the distribution of the water of the Indus and its tributaries between the two countries. It was prepared and negotiated by the World Bank and its stipulations have been more or less scrupulously followed by either side despite all the differences on other issues, conflicts and wars. Under the terms of the Treaty, India has untrammelled use of the three eastern tributaries—Beas, Sutlej and Ravi—while Pakistan has the rights to the waters of the western tributaries—Chenab and Jhelum—and the Indus itself. The latter two tributaries should thus have been different. They were not, however, and the presence of the Mangla Dam perhaps provides the reason in the case of the Jhelum.

Only once did I see the Jhelum in her glory. There may have been a flash flood or a release from Mangla. For whatever reason, the river was in fine flow near the town that bears its name. At the sight of the waters lapping the ghats, which still existed, there welled up in me the reverence Hindus proverbially feel when confronted with a blessing river.

The feeling evoked by the Indus at Attock was altogether different. It was one of awe at real splendour. The Indus here is nowhere as broad as the Brahmaputra is at Tezpur, nor does it give the impression of a massive brooding potential as the Ganga does at Prayag. That far north, the Sindhu has not been joined by her major tributaries and the terrain has not allowed her to spread. The river is still majestic as it curves past the hills of Hazara and the dark bulk of the fort at Attock.

Balochistan remained a land I was unable to enter. But I was more fortunate than most Indians who have visited Pakistan in that I traversed a bit of the North West Frontier Province. The Peshawar plain was somewhat akin to land around Kabul as I was to discover later. That probably had more to do with the settlement patterns of the people living on it than the land itself. What I remember are the thick, high walls of mud surrounding homesteads, water glinting from narrow canals and vegetable plots both bordered by dykes studded with poplars and fruit trees.

Mingora, the gateway to the Swat Valley, was no different in my recollection, though with low buildings climbing the surrounding slopes, this one-time seat of the Wali (or ruler) had a hill station's charm. The Valley was at first glance all that it was cracked out to be. Steep-sided mountains soaring up from the banks of a swift-flowing torrent, its turquoise waters slapping over grey rocks, the slopes covered by the thick green of conifers. As we drove further up-valley, the road snaking by the side of the river, we caught glimpses of the snow that still filled the high crags though it was late summer.

At points on the route, following instructions from the brochures and the occasional signposts, we stopped to admire the remnants of the Gandhara art that had once been the envy of the world. Like a relief of the Buddha sitting in the lotus position, the outlines of the figure still clearly visible, its features obliterated long ago by an idol-hater's axe—a whimsical indicator that a flood tide of iconoclasm had stopped short of total destruction.

This road forms one of the trunks of the Karakoram Highway, much vilified in India when its inauguration was announced since it was supposed to symbolize the unholy alliance between Pakistan and China. Although the highway has a connection with the dispute over Aksai Chin, its re-emergence as a route for Sino-Pak trade and travel should not have come as a surprise. The Swat Valley had been used in the centuries before and after Christ by pilgrims and merchants moving from the land where Buddhism originated to the country where the religion had one of its largest body of adherents. Gandhara art was among the great products of this mingling and we moderns should perhaps consider ourselves fortunate that all traces of the magnificent culture have not been erased.

Over the first two decades of this the twenty-first century, the highway might have lost a bit of its uniqueness as it has been merged into a larger scheme. It is now one of the strands of the vast Belt and Road gridwork that the People's Republic is spreading over the global map. If that scheme is to succeed, the engineering would need to be multiple degrees better than it was in the 1990s. In parts, the road was reduced to long, rubble-strewn strips that threatened to shred the tyres. At others, massive boulders choked the track into obstacle courses through which drivers had to feel their way. So much so that the '*dulhans*', the gaily decorated trucks that regularly ply this route, looked battered and bruised.

Road construction was not the only aspect that called for a major upgrade of engineering skills. Throughout the long sweep of the subcontinent's northern mountain barrier, in all its ranges, local inhabitants have for long depended on the ample timber and stone available on the hillsides for constructing their homes and other buildings. Chemical explosives have made the process much easier but the time saved has not been spent in any form of clean-up or restoration of the environs. In Swat, either because the lay of the land showed up the scars more clearly or because of laxer regulation, the devastation appeared a whole lot worse. Great fallen timbers slanted across cascades of rock slides, the regularity of the debris showing that man and not nature had been at work. Anyone with a little concern for the happiness of future generations and the health of the global environment must hope that someone has taken the initiative to reverse the trend. This is the patch of earth that produced Malala Yusufzai. If someone has taken the lead in fighting for nature as she did for the cause of girls' education, all might not be lost. Make no mistake about it. If the Swat Valley is ruined, every denizen of the world, including Indians of generations yet to be born, will be deprived of a precious part of their common heritage.

The second glance that registers the environmental destruction can easily overwhelm the joy of the first impression. However, a third look revealed Swat's true mystique.

Terraced fields spiralled up the hillsides. Orchards and pine groves provided soothing contrasts to the grey of the wider valley bottomlands with their markets and truck stops. The undisturbed upper reaches remained as testimonials to the legend of Swat's beauty. If any doubts remained, they were dispelled at Kalam, where a high mountain lake surrounded by meadows of thick grass lay untroubled by human encroachment.

Years after that trip of ours, the Swat Valley was to fall into the grip of the Taliban. Pakhtuns of the Yusufzai and other tribes that inhabit the areas are undoubtedly devout. Yet, when I heard the news, I could not get the connect between the memories of the people we had met and the imagery of savage fanaticism that the term Taliban invokes. I remembered the smiling waiter, working at a roadside *dhaba*, wading through an ankle-deep stream to bring us plates of grilled trout that we ate while sitting on charpoys plonked into the water.

Courtesy never flagged even when people realized we were not what they initially thought we were. We asked two tall, dignified gentlemen, who looked like off-duty police or army officers, if we could enter a mosque made entirely of wood. Our question had been put in Urdu and their first response was in the same language. They took a step past, stopped, did a second take and told us very pleasantly in English, 'Please do. It is a place of worship.'

In one of the tourism department guesthouses where we had booked a room, we had to place our order for dinner at lunch time itself. We asked for mutton curry and *roti* and went off to do whatever we had planned. At dinner, they gave us *dal* and *roti* but no mutton. When we asked the waiter what the problem was he said that the butcher only had beef left in his stall when the guesthouse man reached there. '*Aap logon ko hum woh toh nahi khila sakte.*' (We can't serve that to you.)

A group of teachers at a hillside school did not have to face that problem. On our way back from a hike into the hills, we passed the school just as the lunch bell finished ringing. Four male teachers who had spread a cloth on the ground and were just taking out their lunch boxes waved us over. They probably took us for city types and given my complexion they must have concluded that we were from Karachi. Nothing changed when we said we were Indians and the *ghee*-rich *aloo-parathas* and pickle washed down with mountain water made for one of the most delicious meals we had ever eaten.

On that trip we even had an insight into the famous Pakhtun attachment to the rifle. A small group of men were walking down a path. One of them was carrying what I could have sworn (on the basis of imagery from the paperback Westerns I had devoured by the truckload during my youth) was a Winchester from the late 1800s. It was probably neither that old nor manufactured in Connecticut. The far greater likelihood was that it had been made in Darra Adam Khel by a craftsman working to a hundred-year-old model.

Swat was one patch of mountain territory that was relatively more accessible to middle-class Pakistanis. They, in the same manner as us foreigners with restricted visas, must have looked wistfully at the advertisements that would crop up every summer promoting holidays in Chitral, Gilgit and Baltistan further north. We were duty-bound to not seek permission to visit the last two places mentioned since they form part of the territory illegally occupied by Pakistan but the vistas seemed as ruggedly beautiful as those of Ladakh and Zanskar. Rustic polo and the special culture of the Kalash (a Hindu/Animist mountain people) were advertised as the special features of Chitral.

Those who could not afford the flight or were otherwise blocked from the far northern parts had to settle for the Murree hills to beat the summer. For the first two years of our stay in Pakistan, we had access to the bungalow the High Commission maintained in the hill station and some memorable weekends were spent there. (The arrangement came to an end for some reason I can't quite recall.) That was a snug, secure place though there was no real need for protection from holiday crowds as I do not remember ever coming across one. Somehow a fair potion of the town seemed to have escaped the horrors of commercial tourism that was even then scarring Shimla, Mussoorie and Ooty. Perhaps the emergence of Nathia Gali and holiday spots in POK had something to do with it. Those places were outside an Indian's purview.

~

Apart from living with the people when you go to another country, you live with their culture and their land. Both of the latter were of course very different from that of Kerala but Nandini and I were used to the North. Pakistan was in a sense an extension of the familiar in a sort of 'receding' manner. What I mean to say is that the sense of 'sameness' that we felt between Wagah and Lahore was replaced in incremental degree by the sense of the different as we moved further west and north. Up until Attock. Once past the bridge across the Indus we found ourselves in another part of Asia.

On confronting the depth of Pakistan, while being aware that you are politically an alien in the country, the reality of separateness eventually sinks in. It is another country and you begin measuring the differences by referencing the three cultural icons of *roti, kapda* and *makaan*. Of these, the last is the least significant. Perhaps the only real change is that mosques replace gurudwaras as centrepieces of the villages you pass.

Somehow I remember the visuals of people as being less colourful than in India. That is surprising because urban Pakistanis were generally more stylish than Indians in those days with the cut of women's clothing definitely superior.

Burqas were not to blame either since this identity-obscuring costume was not too visible in villages or towns; less ubiquitous than they were in our hometown of Kozhikode. Women preferred *dupattas* that were more usually flung fashionably around shoulders than wrapped around heads.

Perhaps it was the generally brown or grey clothing of the men that gave this impression of colourlessness. They might have preferred to wear *lungis* in their villages and Western clothes to office but had more or less all adopted Awami as the national dress. I found it more roomy and comfortable than *kurta-pyjama* and found it amusing that Pakistani officialdom frowned on Indians wearing it. One major plus point of the Awami was that it was classless. Without close scrutiny of the material used, the economic standing of a person could not be readily assessed.

On a visit to Australia many years later, Matt Preston, the presenter of the programme *Master Chef*, told me during a chat about Indian food, that the flavour of biryani changes every fifty kilometres. That's when I realized a truth about our own cooking. Distances may vary but on a drive from Chennai to Kerala you go through the Ambur, fringes of the Chettinad and Dindigul-Thalaipekettu and then the Kovai biryani zones before you can taste the Malabar variety. To quite an extent, each biryani flavour represents a micro-culture.

Biryani did not seem to be top of the favourite list in Pakistan but the aphorism about distinctions in flavour, however slight, representing a micro-culture seemed to be borne out. Lahori cuisine is not identical to either the

Mughlai or the Punjabi of Delhi even when the choice is limited to non-vegetarian. Meat curries and *dals* are drier and less redolent of the spices we are used to and the contrast deepens as you near Peshawar. Mohajirs had carried with them their techniques of softening meat with papayas so I found the *kababs* in Karachi generally better than in North India though the *chaapli* was a real discovery. Ironically, the most delightful of all were the *naans* baked in tandoors with just the right touch of salt added. (Most markets had *naan* bakeries and one hot from the oven was a meal in itself.)

Given the variations in food, soil, water and climate, the cultures of regions and ethnic groups had perforce to be different from one another. Such broad distinctions were also noticeable when it came to music, preference in colours of clothes and houses, Urdu accents, the work ethic and the *tehzeeb*. (An officer from the Sindh Police Special Branch stopped and quizzed me for a while in Karachi one time. Every question was preceded and followed by a '*Saeen*' and the man pressed a palm to his heart and bowed every time I answered.)

For all the political differences, even hostilities born of conflicting interests, the ethnic groups are no longer strangers to one another. Each could not but have become acquainted with the ways of others since they all travel, work and study in the same country while interaction with foreigners is infrequent. Although it might not have led to brotherly love, the sense of being stuck in the same boat would have created an indifference to idiosyncrasies, if not tolerance.

All this might not amount to a composite culture. However, there does seem to be sufficient commonality as to render efforts to homogenize the people unnecessary, even oppressive.

Forging an Identity

At least some people in India would have heard of the thesis that Mohammed bin Qasim was the sower of the seed that grew to become Pakistan. Nandini taught at the Islamabad Grammar School but though she has a degree in History, the management did not think it prudent that she teach the subject. I do not remember laying my hand on the relevant textbook. However, the more ardent propagators of this myth reiterated it often enough in newspaper articles that I am more or less convinced it did find a place in the curriculum.

From other assertions common in the public discourse, it was apparent that dubious, even downright incorrect, notions about sub-continental history were taken as matters of fact. This myth-making was at its most effulgent when narrating the flow of events from the twelfth century CE. Muslim martial prowess had carried the crescent flag to every corner of South Asia and this banner would have still been flying if not for European intervention. A Shivaji or a Hari Singh Nalwa found an occasional mention though the further elaboration that the Marathas and Sikhs were overlords of the Indus plains for fairly long stretches in the eighteenth and nineteenth centuries did not; except in that 'Sikh shahi' was used as an epithet for a particularly heinous form of despotism.

During their reign, the British were supposed to have favoured the Hindus and suppressed the Muslims. As evidence for this claim, the ousters of Wajid Ali Shah and Bahadur Shah Zafar would be trotted out with no mention of the same being done to the Peshwa and the Rani of Jhansi's son. Further corroboration was supposedly provided by the fact of Muslims being under-represented in the colonial administration. Somehow the community's tardiness in accepting Western education and thus accessing colonial-era jobs was glossed over even when praise was heaped on Sir Syed Ahmed Khan.

Selective presentation of the record became even more rampant as the narrative moved through the termination of the colonial period and on to the years after Independence. That Partition was a universal demand of all South Asian Muslims was an article of faith. Both the resistance to the idea put up until virtually the last minute by the Punjabi Muslim *zamindars* of the Unionist Party and the outright opposition of many in the overwhelmingly Muslim Frontier Province and elsewhere was glossed over. Post-Independence subcontinental history was a litany of Hindu perfidy, treacherousness and cowardice. Mujahid valour had not prevented the breakaway of Bangladesh though it had blocked the total annexation of Kashmir, went the tale. Here, the supposed lessons of history were hammered home with special vehemence as the purpose metamorphosed into one of fortifying the national resolve to fend off an inveterate enemy.

Perhaps the best example of a sponsored myth capturing the public understanding is the Pakistani take on the United Nations Security Council Resolutions pertaining to Jammu and Kashmir. Officialdom in that country knows that certain actions have to be first carried out by their side before conditions can be considered conducive for a plebiscite. Till date there does not appear to have been a single official attempt to lay out this position before the people. Military and civilian leaderships alike have preferred to enshrine the plebiscite as a divine right that is being denied by a treacherous India.

Some of those subjected to this indoctrination seem to have succumbed to it. There are others who have swallowed before rejecting and yet others who have remained immune right through. In some cases parts of the teaching seem to have stuck while other parts have not. Adherence to the doctrine also seems to fluctuate from time to time. Indoctrination does not mix well with hypocrisy and the man on the street often displays an uncanny knack for nailing the truth. Targets for indoctrination are not impressed when they see generals in suits being chauffeured around in limousines or hear about a mullah getting a sandwich massage.

~

While Indians are highly amused when made aware of the Mohammed bin Qasim as originator thesis, the legend has great bearing on Pakistan's sense of itself since religion provides the clearest demarcation between it and the greater mass from which it broke off. The story is that a young Arab commander in the early eighth century established an outpost of the Umayyad Caliphate by capturing a town in Sindh after defeating its Hindu ruler. How this isolated outpost could have blossomed into the sultanates centred on Delhi that first came into being five centuries later was never explained. Mohammed bin Qasim came by ship and planted the seed. Then Muhammed of Ghor came on horseback nearly five hundred years later, resurrected a withered plant and made it into a tree. Even Ali Baba could not have done better!

Such narrative-building would have been more plausible if it had been done with a sense of proportion. It could have been said that bin Qasim was the first to bring into and establish on the subcontinental soil the Arab race with its unique religion, language and culture. (That would not have been true because voyagers from the Persian Gulf were familiar to the people of the west coast from well before the Hijra but we can let that go.) The story could have gone on to the tenth-century raids by Turkic marauders such as Mahmud of Ghazni to illustrate the continuity of contact with the wider Muslim world. The early thirteenth-century enthronement of the Ghurid (or Mamluk) dynasty in Delhi could have been shown, accurately, as the outcome of a long and erratic process.

A more authentic account of this sort was apparently not preferred for a mix of reasons. Pakistanis are well aware that Arabs, Persians and Turks look at them as late, somewhat suspect, converts. At one point during my stint, the then government mooted legislation to strengthen the Shariah code already in force. Even as parliamentarians were pouring out of the National Assembly, an Arab journalist who was believed to have links with the Muslim Brotherhood could be heard proclaiming loudly, 'How can you impose an Islamic system in a Hindu country?' Not a single Pakistani politician or journalist took issue with him.

It was not enough to show that Islam had marked its presence in the subcontinent only a few years after it became established in West Asia. There was a need to gain acknowledgement that this presence was a dominant one. That, therefore, a subcontinental Muslim state had as much antiquarian legitimacy as similar entities elsewhere. From this perspective, Pakistan is an expansion of the eighth-century polity—or the glorious culmination of an unbroken process begun at that time. The purpose is not only to show that this enterprise of creating a state for South Asian Muslims started further back than it actually did but to also tell the Arabs and others, 'Our standing in the faith is as solid as yours.'

A claim of this sort is undermined if it takes into account inconvenient facts such as the existence of counter-currents—championed by Hindus and maybe Buddhists—that confined bin Qasim's successors to a small strip of territory; the reconciliation between the new entrants and the myriad others who had come to the Indus plains before; their joint resistance to Turkic marauders; betrayals on either side that made a mockery of religious identity; and the pillage and rape inflicted by successive invaders on the ancestors of those currently living in the area.

There also seems to be a hope that the myth will somehow help gloss over demographic realities. Bin Qasim leapt to the shore with at best the few hundred men he could have brought on his ships. The Ghaznavids and other raiders may have left a few thousand descendants behind. Ghurids and the Mughals after them might have come in the tens of thousands. But these invasions could have left no more than a sprinkling on top of the few million, at least, who were living in these territories from long before the Common Era. Pakistanis do not need to be students of history to know this truth. Their family traditions, even their names, tell them what races they originated from.

People who have Syed, Khilji, Lodhi, Mirza or Chaghtai in their names can claim descent from the conquerors. Presumably that also gives them claim to superior status either on ecclesiastical grounds (as with the Syeds) or on the imperialist (as with the rest). Although people of these backgrounds are actually associated with conquerors, they have little to gain by blocking other groups from claiming like origins. They can adopt an attitude of amused tolerance since the myth of being associated with conquerors is important to other classes that dominate the state and society. Members of those other classes are the descendants of the people who resisted the 'foreigners' until they were eventually conquered and converted.

Pakistanis of more indigenous descent would say that their ancestors resisted out of ignorance. That the forefathers became staunch adherents of the foreign-sourced religion once they were convinced about its veracity. With this sort of construct, lineages are free to pick any point in time post bin Qasim's arrival as the moment when the light dawned on them. They are thus free to define the depth of their family's roots in Islam.

Until the 1990s at least, Pakistani Rajputs were as assertive of their superiority vis-à-vis other social classes as were their Indian counterparts. If anything they might be even more so now since the Raja-class on this side of the border has been forced to recognize that in a democracy the greater numerical strength of the subalterns neutralizes traditional advantages. A senior member of the Indian High Commission staff once told me about a dinner he had attended at the house of a person of great standing in Pakistan's theatre world. At some point the casual talk veered towards the attitudinal changes that had taken place in Indian cities towards domestic servants.

The Indian diplomat spoke of the ways in which the difficulty of getting domestic help in Delhi had broken down old barriers and said that in his household all castes including Dalits entered the kitchen freely. At this point, the Pakistani was said to have exclaimed, 'We will never allow those [expletive] to enter our kitchens!' Hearsay no doubt, but this was a wholly private chat and the diplomat was not egging me on to a propaganda campaign against Pakistani upper classes.

In India, socio-political upheavals have seen Yadavs, Ahirs and other middle-level castes gain clout matching that of Rajputs. Since a subaltern upsurge of this sort has not occurred across the border, there has been no cause for upper classes there to rethink their position. A trace of this inter-class competition was discernible in Pakistan with the

Jats claiming equal standing, though they always gave the impression that that they were playing catch-up.

Then there were the Awans, Noons, Janjuas, Bhattis and so on of the 'military zone'. This zone essentially comprised the Potohar Plateau (or the Salt Range) and adjoining tracts to the east and west of it. In administrative terminology, these are the Rawalpindi, Gujranwala and Peshawar divisions, which traditionally provided the bulk of the rank and file of the Pakistani armed forces with the Potohar as the prime ground. They were presumably Rajput though they seemed to prefer to be known by their *gotra* or tribal names.

Pakistanis would insist that affiliations of this type are '*biradaris*', not castes. Superficially, and to an extent, they are right, but not in essence. So far as communal prayer and dining are taken as evidence of the absence of caste, the distinction seemed warranted. Marriages across the *biradari* lines did not seem uncommon either, at least in the cities. But to say that there was no consciousness of hierarchy would be false, plain and simple. Scheduled Castes (the term 'Dalit' had not crossed the border at that time) are largely Christian, rejected and oppressed by the dominant communities. Potters, barbers and others on the lower rungs of the traditional hierarchy did not seem to be much better off either.

I do not recall coming across a Pakistani claiming Brahmin descent, though when one looks at surnames, especially among Kashmiris, some clearly had a Hindu priest or two in their lineages. Perhaps that was a matter of embarrassment. With most Pakistani lineages having converted somewhere along the generations, none wanted a reminder that their families were once the upholders of a now abhorrent tradition.

What does caste consciousness have to do with national myth-making? And how did a caste or a group of castes come to impose their worldview on the rest of the country? There is a straightforward answer to the second question. Thereby a preliminary part of the answer to the first as well. Landholdings in Punjab (the province with more clout than the rest put together) did not in the popular reckoning approach the gigantic proportions of Sindhi feudal territories. According to some newspaper reports of the time, Sindhi feudals such as the Pir of Pagaro and Ghulam Mustafa Jatoi did not measure their land in terms of acreage but by counting the number of railway stations situated on them. Still, Punjabi *zamindaris* were by no means insignificant.

In a chat with a few Punjabi bureaucrats whose families farmed, the matter of land reforms in my home state cropped up. While certainly not an expert on the subject, I told them that farmland in Kerala had passed to the hands of the tillers and that ten acres of paddy was considered the norm. They listened with polite curiosity but then summed up with bewilderment and maybe a touch of disdain, '*Assi-sau acre ke bagair kya kheti karoge?*' (What farming can you do without eighty or hundred acres?)

I do not know if fragmentation of holdings across successive generations of families has taken place in West Punjab as it has in the eastern part of the once united province. Even if it has, the idea that '*zamin*' is the true wealth is still probably prevalent. Its grip was certainly strong in the 1990s. At that time, the Sharif family with its sprawling Ittefaq industrial empire was an economic powerhouse. It still needed to buy farmland in Raiwind and its members had to show that they spent their weekends there in order to cement their social standing.

Feudal status might itself have been a sufficient condition for enabling Rajputs and similar landholding classes to impose their worldview on other segments of society in all provinces. A particular trajectory of history enabled Punjabi landholders to do more. They began joining the officer cadre of the armed forces once the British provided 'natives' the opportunity to do so. Come Partition and the ascent of the military to the pinnacle of power in the country, the Punjabi landholding class was in a position to impose its worldview on the country as a whole. Today, scions of the traditional feudal families might have been supplanted to a large extent by officers hailing from humbler backgrounds. But the strains of the '*zamindari*' culture must still be quite strong given the rural roots of most military men.

The story of how a particular ethos came to dominate the Pakistani military and thereby the country is an interesting one. Until 1857, the British Indian Army, especially its Bengal Native Infantry contingent, was made up mainly of the Rajputs and Bhumihars of the Gangetic plain. After the Sepoy Mutiny (this term is more appropriate in this context than the phrase 'First War of Independence'), Punjab became the main base for recruitment. At Partition, Hindus and Sikhs opted for India while the Punjabi Mussalman joined the armed forces of the new dominion. They formed almost the entirety of the armed forces with Pakhtuns making for the bulk of the remainder. Even among the Punjabi Mussalmans, the men from the Potohar Plateau had the pride of place (and reputedly still do). This configuration set the condition for another twist in the moulding of the national worldview.

One of the most pernicious pieces of intellectual baggage the British foisted on the subcontinent is the theory of the martial races. Which caste group or community fell into this category changed as the colonialists made their way northward and westward. So much so that the very people who helped them conquer Punjab and Sindh—the Bhumihars and Rajputs of Awadh and Bihar—were struck off the list after they rebelled in 1857. Punjabis became the martial race from then on and the Pakistani army, to go by the mass of commentary from military men and civilians alike, sees itself as the purest repository of the warrior spirit.

The martial race obsession can take weird forms. In the course of what can be described as a 'warm discussion' at the Karachi Press Club, one of the disputants argued that while India had several martial races, Pakistan was full of them. Then he asked me, 'What are Menons anyway? Brahmins?'

My spine straightened, shoulders shot back, chin went up and I barked, 'No! Nair.'

He looked nonplussed as could have been expected and asked me what Nairs were. I did not need to respond directly. The answer was provided by a wizened older scribe who seemed to have studied the matter in greater depth.

'They are a martial race as good as yours, you Rajput bugger.'

As the above exchange reveals, 'non-martial' Pakistanis can treat the theory with as much exasperation, even derision, as their counterparts on this side of the border. There is a vital difference though. Due to a conscious decision to go for 'all-class' recruitment and the entry of all manner of tough peasant stock from Mahars and Mazhabis to Santhals and Nagas, the Indian armed forces are quite transformed from what they were in 1947. Over seven decades, the defence services in our country have come to look on themselves as hardened professionals who implement policy formulated by the constitutionally-authorized elected governments. Professionals the Pakistani servicemen might be, but other transformative influences seem to have passed them by. A homogeneous ethos tends to stifle mental expansion.

With almost a third of the pre-Partition military establishment giving its allegiance to Pakistan, the new dominion faced a massive imbalance between institutions. It found itself stuck with a defence apparatus that was grossly disproportionate to its needs and capacity. The armed forces were also the only properly organized body with a patriotic agenda that set it apart. Although the military had also served the imperialists, it seems to have acquired a national spirit faster than a very rickety bureaucracy. There was little competition from political forces either since the Muslim League was not, in organizational spread and muscle, in the same league as the Indian National Congress. Through the combination of these factors, Pakistan from inception was on the way to becoming a state at the service of its army.

Many Pakistani commentators were to later lament that their country could have gone on another trajectory if either Mohammed Ali Jinnah had lived a bit longer or the first Prime Minister Liaquat Ali Khan had not been assassinated. Their deaths left a vacuum that other civilian leaders were not able to fill. As the only organized force with a distinct outlook, which also had the respect of the people, the Pakistani military decided within a decade that it had the duty and the wherewithal to shape the nation's character and plan its future. Four generations of Pakistanis have suffered the disastrous consequences of their military's misjudgement of its own capabilities. More unforgivably, so have four generations of Indians.

~

A former Indian defence attaché in Pakistan, Major General G.K. Duggal, Vir Chakra (that was his rank then but he was to retire as Director General of Assam Rifles with the rank of Lieutenant General), had a pithy way of summing up the problem: 'You know, these Punjabis [on the other side of the border]. They'll come roaring at you and when you punch them in the nose, they will go away just as fast.'

Our own Punjabi infantryman emphasized the last part of his statement for understandable reasons. But the first part seems just as accurate. Since 1947, every successive generation of Pakistani generals appears to have embarked on a misadventure against India almost as if it was a rite of passage. That they have been sent scuttling on every occasion is not the point. The nonsense about martial races and what it means for the measurement of yourself and the other seems to have quite a bit to do with this persistent urge to provoke a much bigger adversary.

Most Indians are probably unaware that the Pakistani

take on the 1947 and 1965 wars is the direct opposite of ours. In their version, both were instances when the weak and cowardly, but perfidiously cunning Hindus, launched aggressions in pursuit of their illegitimate objective of annexing Kashmir. Supposedly, the infidel hordes were thwarted only because the valiant Pakistanis put up a heroic defence though inferior in numbers and materiel. Something on the same lines was trotted out about the 1971 war, albeit with the necessary plot alteration to account for the loss of East Pakistan/Bangladesh and the capture of 93,000 of its soldiers. From the little I could follow in the Pakistan press at the time of the Kargil conflict, this assessment continued to have a shelf life.

Accounts of one's own history put out by institutions are usually not of much value unless corroborations are available from other sources. In Pakistan's case the lack of corroboration does not discredit the tale because of the dearth of questioning by most people inside that country. That too might not have mattered to us if the yarn-spinning had not been used to consistently and continuously build and sustain hostility towards India. The effects of these propagandizing efforts are surprisingly pervasive as the following anecdote will bear out.

Asif Ali Zardari was making what veteran observers felt was the first major speech he made in the National Assembly. For most of the time between mid-1990 and mid-1993, Zardari was in jail pending trial on a host of charges. He was on one of the paroles allowed to him so that he could attend parliament and was using the opportunity to assert the patriotism of the Sindhis.

The thrust of Zardari's argument was that Punjabis could contemplate peace with India 'since the Sikhs were their brothers'. Sindhis, on the other hand, could not take a step in this direction because Hindus were enemies. Why were the Hindus so horrible? Because, according to Zardari, they resorted to low cunning to cheat the Muslims. Then he turned to the member from Umarkot to ask whether this was not true. Zardari was not challenging Rana Chander Singh to refute his statement. Bizarre as it may sound, he was actually asking the ruler of the Hindu Rajput state to support his assertion.

Given this attempt to rope in the Rana, it must not be assumed that Benazir's husband was distinguishing between Pakistani Hindus and their Indian co-religionists. He was actually playing to a long prevalent theme that Hindus are basically *Banias* who can never be trusted by the landed classes. There is a history to the emergence of this perspective. Before Partition, because of the Islamic injunction against levying interest, members of the community did not indulge in any form of banking. They had to turn to Hindu moneylenders for loans and the fear of foreclosures was widespread. While bankers became objects of hatred and dread, the Rana as a landholder was obviously on the right side of the fence.

By the way, the pundits who thought well of Zardari's intervention did not seem to find anything amiss. If they had any inkling of its 'political incorrectness', they gave no indication. That the speech denigrated sections of their own citizenry did not seem to occur to people whose democratic credentials were otherwise not in doubt.

This is such a basic comparison problem stemming from

wrong images about the Self and the Other. A really weird conceptualization of the world survives because it goes unchallenged. Bar the handful of Parsis, there were hardly any minorities with the social and economic standing to assert that their communities were made of people with myriad tastes and capabilities.

~

Martial pretensions seem to have meshed with a communalized reading of subcontinental history. The theory apparently is that the martial valour of the ancestors got so sharpened by religious faith after their conversion that Muslims were able to dominate the whole of the subcontinent by the end of Aurangzeb's reign. Or, in the version preferred by the most zealous, the whole subcontinent had become Pakistan by 1707 CE.

Left out of such a reading of history is a fundamental incongruity. The territory within which Pakistan currently exists and the people who lived on it in times past were overrun by every invader from the East and the West. Mauryas, Guptas, Marathas, Sikhs and the English had moved in from one direction while the Greeks (or Macedonians), Persians, Huns, Shakas, Mongols, Turks and Afghans had entered from the other.

The true state of affairs was once graphically brought out by the Najibullah regime's ambassador in Islamabad. While I was chatting with him during a party at the Indian High Commission, he was approached by a group of Pakistani journalists who told the Ambassador that it would be great if his country become part of theirs. The Ambassador replied, 'I am sorry my friend but you have got your history wrong. Afghanistan has never been a part of Pakistan while your country has often been made a part of mine.'

Communalized interpretations of the past are a necessary part of the endeavour to provide the state with a religious identity. To go by what seems the most reasonable historiography, the leaders of the Pakistan movement never thought that they were laying the foundations of a theological state. Jinnah's first address after becoming Governor-General has over time become a much-quoted document since it amounts to a mission statement. Taken together with the accounts of his character and the worldview of the core cadre of the Muslim League, a theocratic system did not figure in their dreams for the future. This outlook seems to have been shared by the oligarchs of the Unionist Party—the party of the landed gentry in pre-Partition Punjab—whose late subscription to the idea of Pakistan made Partition possible. Most League leaders were from provinces that were to remain in India and had no roots in the new country. Those roots were provided by Muslim landlords—Feroz Khan Noon, Mumtaz Daulatana, etc.—who discarded their Unionist affiliations and plumped wholly for the League in the mid-1940s.

In summarizing a long, complicated, convoluted process, it seems fair to say that Jinnah and associates had a template of a sovereign state that would serve as a haven for people who wanted to keep alive the Muslim cultural ethos of the subcontinent while leaving the non-Muslims within it unhindered. Another element of the plan was that the predominant religion and the social practices associated with it would be given due respect, even pre-eminence, but within limits. Such limits were never specified though they could perhaps have been extrapolated from the lines in Jinnah's speech that the constitutional, political and civic rights of citizens would not be defined on the basis of religious identity or strength of affinity to it.

Let alone the minorities, even most Pakistani Muslims do not appear to have shaken off their bewilderment at the souring of this promise. Rational commentators apart, even most ordinary citizens seemed to instinctively know that theocracy had never been part of the original project. As the record shows, parties such as the Jamaat-e-Islami, which have stood for a theocratic model, have never got anything more than marginal shares of the vote. Even in casual conversations, ordinary citizens often made evident their view that theocratic elements had been brought into the state system through the back door. They were not too enthusiastic about accepting a religion-based model of governance even in the early 1990s, when the country was emerging from the shadow of a piety-obsessed dictator. For the preceding decade, Zia and his mullah cohorts had given the Pakistani masses a thorough working over as part of the effort to turn Jinnah's dream into a nightmare. Liberal-minded Pakistanis believe that their interpretation of Jinnah's message is the authentic one and that it should and could prevail given the right circumstances.

Indians, who have grown up with the belief that Jinnah was the evil genius of Partition, might find it strange that he should now be presented as a paragon of liberalism. Lal

Krishna Advani was one man who got punished for uttering such a blasphemy. Still, if we can somehow excise Jinnah's Partition politics as we reassess him, there is no denying that this urbane Bar-at-Law was indeed a liberal; certainly more of one than many of his successors.

From the above it should not be presumed that Pakistan would have automatically become a fair, democratic-minded nation if Zia had never ruled. Except for the vocal set of human rights activists and the bolder sections of the media, hardly anyone ever raised a protest when the state apparatus including the judiciary violated the rights of minority citizens in the most grotesque of ways. Perhaps, to be extra charitable, this apathy was born out of an awareness of futility. Or perhaps, as is more likely, it was a product of the instinct for self-preservation.

It is possible to think of yet another explanation. Human and civil rights need to attain a certain level of buoyancy in a society as a whole before they become available to all its members. Take the plight of transgender people in India. The injustice they have suffered for centuries, if not forever, is blatantly visible and always has been. No one spared them a thought until other sections—religious minorities, Dalits, Adivasis—started exercising their rights. It was only after the assertion of rights by other traditionally oppressed people had attained some critical mass that the judiciary began granting the LGBTQ community its due.

When a state does not grant fundamental liberties to any of its people, or restricts rights severely, there are really no advantaged sections to take up the cause of the disadvantaged. Without allies and some fighting space, it is very difficult for the downtrodden to break free. It is the kind of condition that leads to bizarre episodes. Among such is the one involving the Christian boy who saw a man sodomizing a donkey and reported it. By the time the police and magistracy processed the investigation, the case had turned on its head. The ass-lover was exonerated while the boy was left facing charges of blasphemy and the imminent danger of a death sentence.

~

The hated Other appeared on the scene early enough in the life of Pakistan. Two sets of minorities—Hindus and Sikhs—could be readily assailed as agents of India. The third—the Christians—were the ideological descendants of the Crusaders who, reappearing as imperialists, had destroyed the Mughal empire and extinguished Muslim glory. After Partition, the Ahmadiyyas were deprived of Muslim status, and throughout the 1990s, yet another section appeared to be on the verge of entering the hit list of the Sunni majority. A senior Iranian journalist pulled no punches when I asked him to identify the root cause of tension between his country and its eastern neighbour. 'On any day now they could declare that Shias are kaffirs,' he said with vehemence.

Zia-ul-Haq is, of course, credited with authorship of the project to intertwine the martial and Islamic identities. His emphasis was perhaps more on the religious rather than the racial or caste aspect. Zia being an Arain (Teli or oil-presser caste in India) and therefore of lesser warrior pedigree than many others serving in the armed forces probably felt that faith would serve his purpose better than caste. He was also reputedly more religious than the rest of the coterie of generals over whom he presided. Whatever might have been the origins, the fusing of the martial and the Islamic was an ongoing project in the 1990s even though Zia had already had his tryst with the mango crates. (The explosive that blew up his aircraft and killed him was apparently hidden amidst the fruit he had been gifted.)

Circumstances seemed to favour the project. The link-up between the oil wealth of the Saudi royal house and the missionary zeal of Wahhabism had taken place many decades before. But the Soviet invasion of Afghanistan and the American entry into the 'Great Game'—replacing the Russian and British empires, respectively, in the struggle for control of Central Asia being waged since the nineteenth century—gave this tie-up added relevance and potency. The anti-Soviet combine made of US weaponry, Islamic fervour and Saudi wealth had to find a base near the frontline of the war. What could possibly be more suitable than Pakistan? For Pakistan, by then under Zia's control, there would be no better opportunity.

With the withdrawal of Soviet forces in 1989, the collapse of the Communist regime in Kabul appeared imminent. Although declarations of victory had to be postponed for three years, the combined efforts of the international coalition seemed close to fruition. Saudi Arabia had provided most of the money and the United States the necessary weaponry but Pakistan was eager to claim that it had played the major role in the victory against the Godless. It seemed to have swallowed its own propaganda that its religious-martial ethos had supplied the real steel to the enterprise.

Kashmir had by then been brought to the boil and General Headquarters (GHQ) seemed to believe that once the spear-thrust was shifted from the west to the east, the Valley would fall into Pakistan's possession. Whether the Generals actually took their own projections seriously or not, their many minions among opinion makers actively promoted this line of thought. The envisioning of wider vistas did not stop there either. Some dream-merchants spoke or wrote about the prospects of spreading the fervour into Central Asia. Almost as if the revival of a Timurid empire, though one centred on Rawalpindi, was round the corner.

Mullahdom was very actively engaged in the propagation of such expansionist fantasies. Most Pakistanis are oriented towards what is called the Barelvi tendency, treating *dargahs* as major focal points of their devotion. But the military seemed to have found stauncher allies among the Deobandi organizations whose *madrasas* supplied the cannon-fodder for the Afghan and Kashmir jihads. The jihadists not only garnered the funds and arms that boosted their political clout and nuisance value, they also used their new status as adjuncts of the military to set themselves up as the purveyors of its ideology.

(It is one of the bitter ironies of history that a theological strain that had opposed the creation of Pakistan could acquire the standing to shape its soul. A further irony is that an army comprised overwhelmingly of men from the Barelvi belt relies on the Deobandis for most of its wet work.)

Mullah claims and pretensions notwithstanding, there were levels beyond which they would not be allowed to ascend. It might be foolhardy to dismiss the possibility of a religious fanatic or cabal taking control of Pakistan's armed forces but the trend-line of Army chiefs who have succeeded Zia suggests that the threat has been kept at bay. From Mirza Aslam Beg, through Asif Janjua, Waheed Kakar, Jehangir Karamat, Pervez Musharraf, Ashfaq Kiyani, Raheel Sharif to Qamar Bajwa and Asim Munir, the person who has occupied the main chair in Rawalpindi has been a non-fanatical professional.

Professionalism and religious moderation does not by any means translate into softness towards India. Far from it. No Pakistani Chief of Army Staff for the foreseeable future is going to stray an inch from the core of the institution's worldview. Bellicosity towards India does not only permeate the military's belief system according to everyone who has studied the 'Afwaj' in depth, it is essential if the institution is to retain its predominance over the state, secure its budget from public scrutiny and protect the Foundations that look after its personnel post-retirement. For a military that possesses the hardware and organizational strength to suppress all possible challengers, an ideological tool is a useful extra. It can demand the forgiveness of all sins because it is the bulwark against Indian aggrandisement, is the bottom line.

A natural offshoot of this mindset is the adoption of a belligerent swagger whenever India comes up as a topic. Pakistani military men seem to take great pride in talking about 'plucking out the eyes of those who cast evil looks at us' or other phrases of the sort. Together with the suppression of the truth that all their wars against India have ended in defeat, this swagger seems intended to fulfil some deepfelt need. It all comes across as an attempt to reassure the masses that there is definitely one sphere in which their country can match its neighbour no matter how wide the gap may be in other fields. Such posturing does seem to offer a measure of comfort for people outside military circles as well.

That does not mean, however, that the citizens of the country are unable to see the patches in the emperor's clothes. There has always been a flock of critics ready to lampoon the Guardians. Their voices become all the louder and their sarcasm the more pungent every time the military suffers a setback. The mockery rang loud and clear when troops were sent to the United Arab Emirates instead of Saudi Arabia or Kuwait during the first Gulf War. 'What are the holy places in Dubai?' was one of the questions asked. Derision was just as sharp when the Mujahideen—but not Rawalpindi's Mujahideen—took control of Kabul in 1992. It probably was as strident after the Kargil war, the toppling of the Taliban in 2002, the killing of Osama bin Laden and the new Kabul regime's rejection of Rawalpindi's tutelage post August 2021.

A story about Zia's times can perhaps serve as the apt metaphor for the success or otherwise of the attempt to impose the ideology on the common man. The late dictator apparently had ordered that all public servants must line up together for the noon *namaaz* on working days. Attendance was said to have been a hundred per cent at the beginning. As time went on, the congregations would start leaking from the rear ranks. So much so that there would be no more than a couple of lines behind the devout dictator by the end of the prayer. Indians might be tempted to take comfort that so many walked away. They would do well to remember that the most ambitious and therefore probably the most determined stayed in place.

~

Is an ideology so layered with hostility to another really necessary? Or, since it is not going to be forsaken because it serves the interests of powerful elements, is it sustainable? A resounding 'Yes' would probably be the response from those who promote the outlook and quite a number beyond them as well. But in real terms? Will even the Chinese risk large investments in a country that misses no opportunity to provoke a more powerful neighbour?

As a country that is constantly leaking intellectual as well as financial capital, Pakistan needs to confront this question.

Lastly, can a people maintain such levels of hostility without doing damage to their collective mental health? Common sense suggests that such damage will occur. An individual who persists with a very negative outlook towards another for a long period runs the risk of making that hostility the definition of himself. Can this not happen to a whole society when its members mutually reinforce this mindset? Such negativity surely must retard a society's growth as much as it does that of an individual.

Flame Carriers

Yogendra Kumar, at that time a First Secretary in the Indian High Commission whose tasks included media monitoring, once told me a story as amusing as it was insightful. 'Yogi' was trying to probe the reason for the intense hostility that the Urdu-paper *Nawa-i-Waqt* and its English counterpart *The Nation* harboured towards India. To this end he put the question to Nusrat Javed, the top political correspondent of that publishing chain.

'Majid Nizami,' Nusrat said, referring to the elder of the two brothers who ran the newspapers, 'is so anti-India that if the whole of your county becomes Muslim, he will become a Hindu.'

Amusement aside, the story serves as a much needed reminder that the streak of hostility towards India that runs through the Pakistani psyche does not really need a sponsor or constant nurturing. It exists, period. Its intensity or width of spread is impossible to gauge since even opinion surveys are very unlikely to give an accurate reading. When animosity is the officially approved default setting, people polled will tend to give what they believe are expected answers.

To go by the general tone in the media and the public discourse, hostility to India was intense and widespread. In the absence of indications to the contrary, it does seem valid to believe that the media and other opinion makers were accurately reflecting public attitudes. On the other hand, quite a bit of the anecdotal evidence as came my way and the application of common sense did suggest otherwise. Most people I interacted with treated me normally once the introductory phase was over. Also, people who have other things to do need to modulate their hatred if for no other reason than to keep their sanity.

There were times when I toyed with the idea of approaching Majid Nizami, sizing him up across halls in which we both happened to be present. The 'don't approach' vibes were unmistakable whenever our eyes met and so I did not. That did not prevent *The Nation* from running in its weekend magazine the full piece I wrote for *Frontline* on Ahmad Shah Massoud's conquest of Kabul. My name was conveniently changed from Kesava to Kesara, but who's making a fuss about a bit of plagiarism between enemies. (After all, the Kesara might have been chosen to convey the message that 'whatever will be, will be'.)

~

There were three avowedly anti-India figures with whom I had weirdly mixed experiences. One was Liaqat Baloch, Member of the National Assembly and bigwig in the political arm of the Jamaat-e-Islami. Baloch was about the safest bet in Pakistan. You would never lose money if you placed it on him to make the fieriest anti-India speech in parliament or outside.

We gradually became acquainted as I took notes at his press conferences or asked him for copies of statements or recorded the Jamaat's response to some development or the other. Even though we never became particularly friendly, over time we started seeing the professional in the other. He certainly was a professional politician who knew when to pull out the rhetoric and when to put out something sensible. More to the point, we each knew where the other stood. Our antagonism, stemming from diametrically opposite philosophies, was so steel bright and strong that we did not have to blur it with petty bickering.

The second epitome of an anti-India Pakistani that I have in mind is none other than Dr Nuke, the father of the Islamic bomb, Abdul Qadeer Khan. He was also the first person who made me realize that extreme cunning can make up for a complete lack of intellect. Although I never had a one-to-one encounter with him, I was part of the paparazzi scrum that crowded around him on the few occasions when he made an appearance at a general gathering. He seemed incapable of stringing two abstract thoughts together.

At that time, A.P.J. Abdul Kalam's star was on the rise in India and AQ seemed to be obsessively envious of it. Apropos of nothing he would boast that he had a real PhD while APJ's was honorary. That would be one sentence. Then another would be about his getting Pakistan the bomb. Then something about Pakistan having now become invincible. Three or four disjoined sentences with no coherence, no relevance to the questions asked of him and no pretence that this was part of a practiced art of avoidance. The man never had anything else to say and he had absolutely no sense of humour.

While I will stick with the above assessments in any circumstances, this portrayal should not make people forget how diabolically shrewd the man was. With Pakistan having nothing of the sort of infrastructure that India had in the nuclear field, A.Q. Khan was able to bring it on par at the finish line. It must have taken an unbelievable degree of single-mindedness and total behavioural control to have cheated, lied and thieved all over the world to build up the bomb-making apparatus.

A Dutch court had sentenced him in absentia on charges of nuclear smuggling for illegally taking away designs and other details pertaining to centrifuges. (Arrays of centrifuges made of a special steel are essential for uranium enrichment.) This verdict was overturned on a technicality when he appealed and further investigations seem to have stalled. However, when the International Atomic Energy Agency probed the nuclear activities of Libya and Iran many years later, it found that Khan had been one of the clandestine suppliers of banned material. It also found that the centrifuges in the possession of Libya and Iran had the design specifications of the Dutch equipment Khan had been accused of illegally copying many years ago.

That all this was years before the Chagai tests did not stop anyone from treating the nuclearization of Pakistan as an accomplished fact. Least of all AQ, and he had extracted his reward for it. The boundary wall of his house on the Margalla Road must have been one of the longest in that poshest of sectors in Islamabad. To judge by the distant slope of the roof there must have been a couple of acres between the building and the perennially closed gates. From the news that came out over a decade later that Dr Nuke had sold his secrets to North Korea and Libya, it is pretty obvious that AQ never thought that the bounty bestowed by his own country was enough. Under pressure from the international community, the regime of Pervez Musharraf in 2004 made AQ confess on television that he had run a proliferation network.

How AQ got away despite causing massive damage to his country's reputation and some harm to its interests remains a mystery. Other than house arrest until his demise, he does not seem to have suffered any punishment. The US, in normal circumstances, could have been expected to push Pakistan to come down hard on a person who had empowered two or three of its enemies. Even without such pressure, the Musharraf regime would have been expected to act against a man who had dealt with national secrets and national assets in such cavalier fashion.

The Musharraf regime might have refrained from tougher action for two possible reasons. For one, AQ by then had been so lionized as the 'Father of the Bomb' that even the military dictator was unable to take further action for fear of a public backlash. Secondly, in a country where little happens without the military's intelligence arm coming to know of it, people in positions of power could have been complicit in the Khan network and they might have needed to buy his silence with a light sentence.

When he spoke on the occasions I have mentioned of

his success in bringing Pakistan to nuclear parity with India, AQ seemed to talk with the fervour of a person trying to convert others to his point of view rather than with pride. It was almost as if he wanted to convince his audience that he was deserving of the rewards given to him. Or, given the revelations about the Khan nuclear network that were to emerge later, perhaps he was trying to convince listeners that he merited more.

Where Liaqat Baloch's anti-India fervour was fuelled by true belief and A.Q. Khan's by avarice, I was totally befuddled by the third person I intend to present here. Lt Gen Hamid Gul had just about ended his military career when I first met him at some function. From 1987 to '89 he had been Director General, Inter-Services Intelligence (ISI) and the main bogeyman for India as well as a whole host of Pakistanis. Although he had been given command of II Corps in Multan after his tenure as spy chief, Gul continued to be the main propagator of the jihadi ideology that ISI and a good chunk of the regular officer cadre had apparently internalized by this time. II Corps, headquartered in Multan, is a strike formation and its command is hence very prestigious. Gul was so keen on his jihad-guiding role that he seemed to prioritize that over his new command. Most professional soldiers prefer command of field units over anything else and Gul was definitely an oddball in this regard, as in so much else.

My first surprise was to discover that the spymaster with an ogre's reputation was actually about the same size as me. The second was that he was soft not only in speech but, from what I could make out, in physique as well. Thirdly,

I was led to suspect that the man was not altogether there, because his first response to me was totally disconcerting. With one of my hands gripped in one of his and the other arm draped on my shoulder he asked me whether it would not be wonderful if India and Pakistan could resolve the Kashmir issue and get along like the friends they were meant to be.

All that was fairly standard spiel though not really expected from the man who had pioneered (according to both Indian agencies and himself) the sending of holy warriors across the LOC. What was totally unexpected was the teary-eyed earnestness with which he expressed these sentiments. Did he really believe that I would be taken in by the entreaty? More to the point, did the man think that convincing one Indian journalist about his sincerity would make a whit of a difference?

Gul never failed to acknowledge me after that. I do not think we ever got within talking distance of each other apart from that singular encounter. But on a few occasions he saw me walking along Islamabad's tree-lined avenues as he whizzed by in his chauffeured SUV and never failed to wave. Brush-ups against Pakistani intelligence men were not usually pleasant and I could not ever figure out Gul's real game.

Post retirement Gul seemed to have intensified his ideology-spreading activities, if the large number of interviews and lectures available on YouTube are anything to go by. There he can be heard banging away on the theme that the warrior spirit of Islam had revived and would sweep all before it. This would be the punchline no matter the topic under discussion. If nothing else, these performances seem to have helped Gul retain the post of head ideologue until his death in 2015.

While on the subject of Hamid Gul, I would like to air a question that has been bothering me for a while. Why do we call it Pakistani-sponsored terrorism? There is nothing 'sponsored' about it, no outsourcing to another party. It is directly controlled, deliberate action by a department of the government. According to a ton of evidence gathered over three decades, except for a minority that had gone across the LOC for training, most of these 'jihadists' are not even from the Valley or the hill tracts fringing the Jhelum's banks. Many are from areas deep inside Pakistan. This is confirmed by the Jammu and Kashmir Police, central armed police forces, military intelligence, the Intelligence Bureau, RAW, NIA, etc. The evidence includes radio intercepts, documents lifted from killed or captured militants, interrogation records, confessions by militants from the Valley themselves who returned to the mainstream, Kashmiri politicians who have picked up information from the ground, Pakistani news reports of wells and schools in South Punjab being named after jihadis, and statements by Hamid Gul and others about youth having gone to fight the jihad to restore Pakistan's glory and so on. The evidence was finally so compelling that Pakistan was put on the watch list of countries that source financial aid for terrorists by the Financial Action Task Force, the global terrorism financing watchdog.

As brought out during the trial of Ajmal Kasab, a branch of the military recruits men in their late teens or early twenties; trains, arms and provides them with supplies; gives them artillery cover when they penetrate; and controls and commands their actions in the field. These young men are full-time, paid employees.

This mode of action is exactly what Pakistan would adopt if it were using teams of the Special Services Group. These are operations being carried out by commandos trained, equipped and tasked like any special forces. Where is the need to give them any other appellation than Pakistani terror operators?

~

Flame carriers such as Nizami and Gul might not have been able to spread the fire of hostility with the relative ease that they did if combustible material had not been readily available. Let us not forget that there were many families that had to flee from East Punjab and further afield in 1947. For example, Zia-ul-Haq's people were from Jalandhar, the Sharifs from a village near Amritsar and Musharraf's from Delhi. Partition-time horrors would be as much part of the lore of these families as of those that fled eastward. In case anybody had forgotten, the official media would do its best to revive memories.

Every August, when I was there, PTV would run tele-dramas in which Hindus and Sikhs would be shown plotting against innocent Muslims. As the anniversaries of the wars of '47, '65 and '71 drew near, newspapers would begin carrying narratives of the deeds of Major Raja Aziz Bhatti and others who had won the Nishan-e-Haider, their highest gallantry award. We in India do likewise though I think we focus more on the heroism and exercise a little more restraint in spewing venom at the other. Or at least we used to, until certain channels decided that postures of hysterical animosity were a better business proposition.

It was like an incessant replaying of the arguments for Partition. That Muslims of the subcontinent are a people apart who cannot live with the Hindus. (Conveniently forgotten in the process is the fact that the creation of Bangladesh showed that some Muslims cannot live with other Muslims.) Developments in Kashmir—that is, the insurgency that had recently broken out—were adduced as evidence of this proposition and also as proof that India had slid irretrievably into depravity. Shortly after the insurgency erupted, opposition parties in Pakistan had taken up this issue to open a new front against the Bhutto government. With barely concealed encouragement from the establishment, Sharif and others began rallying masses behind the charge that the government was not doing enough for the cause. Benazir soon took up the cause herself and her speeches at mass meetings, punctuated by cries of 'Azadi, Azadi', came as a shock to an India accustomed to thinking of her as a peacenik.

Benazir was dismissed from her first premiership soon after I took on my assignment and Pakistan moved into election mode without much further ado. As brought out subsequently, it appears that Gul and his cohorts in the domestic intelligence wing of ISI had made much headway towards setting up a pro-establishment alliance, called Islami Jamhoori Ittehad, to take on the PPP. This alliance, which included the Pakistan Muslim League and the Jamaat-e-Islami, claimed the stronger nationalist credentials and thereby the greater commitment to the 'liberation of Kashmir'. If I remember right, the term jihad had not come into vogue but the cause of 'Azadi' was the prime election issue.

IJI rallies could be menacing. For one, they were almost entirely masculine affairs and guns were very much on display. With several League stalwarts hailing from the Potohar, large numbers from the military zone attended the Islamabad rallies and the intent to crush the PPP's non-patriotic Jiyalas—'devotees'—was unmistakeable. For instance, no one seemed to notice the irony in giving full-throated support to the slogan 'Mard-e-Momin, Mard-e-Haq! Zia-ul-Haq, Zia-ul-Haq!' Cheers for a deceased dictator at a democratic function!

The PPP's defensiveness was visceral. Already on the back foot for a poor record of governance during their two-year incumbency, Benazir's party also seemed to have conceded the lead on the 'Azadi for Kashmir' issue. Perhaps they felt physically intimidated. A rally in a medium-sized square in Rawalpindi (possibly the same one where she was assassinated on 27 December 2007) was an eye-opener. It was packed, and as was usual with this party's rallies, the faithful were asked to join in on the chorus of songs praising its founder Zulfiqar Ali. At the end of each stanza the singer would break into the refrain, 'Nara-e-Bhutto, Nara-e-Bhutto' ad infinitum, and the crowd would respond with overhead handclaps and the chant of 'Jiye, Jiye, Jiye Bhutto'.

Then three young men got onto the stage and started dancing in tight circles, chanting '*Ya Khuda, Ya Rasool, Benazir Beqasoor*' (O God, O Prophet, Benazir is innocent).

Suddenly, from one of the floors of an under-construction building abutting the square, a stentorian voice bellowed an unbelievably filthy obscenity. The crowd froze. Some young men seemed ready to take issue with the shouter but were held back by others. That unfinished building and a couple of roofs nearby were packed with other men and there seemed reason to believe that there were lots of guns, maybe even grenades, up there.

With the IJI comfortably winning the National and Punjab provincial Assembly polls, another pro-establishment alliance of PPP dissidents under Jam Sadiq Ali and the Mohajir Qaumi Movement capturing Sindh, the forces fully committed to the Kashmir insurgency had brought all levers of power under their control. The military and the Presidency had fostered the policy in the first place and they now had the elected government and, presumably the people, aligned alongside. Restraint on anti-India sentiment was virtually non-existent pre-election. After the IJI victory it flared bright and strong for well over a year.

From the fact that the anti-India rhetoric did not continue to stay at the fever-pitch it attained in 1991, it should not be presumed that it abated significantly. Trouble within the IJI–Presidency–military triumvirate, setbacks in Afghanistan, shock at India's ability to contain the insurgency among other factors contributed to the relative dampening of fervour for the Kashmir cause. However, this cycle has occurred before and major failures—as in 1947–48 and 1965—served only to lift the issue from the hotplate for a decade or two. About that amount of time has elapsed since the last attempt in 1999 and while we Indians might like to believe that the lessons from the misadventures have been learnt, we need to remember that Pakistan has not changed its position. Issues that have agitated the Kashmiris since the 1980s have not been resolved and flare-ups on this side could incite stepped-up involvement from across the border.

Officially, Pakistan maintains that it only extends moral, diplomatic and political support to the Kashmiris. That trained people and war-making material continue to be sent across the LOC, however, is confirmed by evidence collected from militants killed or captured in the Valley (and the Rajouri–Poonch hill regions). According to the reports that appear from time to time Pakistan has off and on placed men such as Masood Azhar, Hafiz Saeed and Zakiur Rehman Lakhvi under house arrest. But it has refused to take further action though their involvement in terrorism appears to have been tacitly acknowledged by these incarcerations.

Although the ongoing suspension of bilateral exchanges was the result of an Indian decision, discussions on outstanding issues were really not going anywhere even before. Of the four outstanding issues, differences pertaining to the Sir Creek and Wullar Barrage concern economic development, while the dispute over possession of the Siachen Glacier is of course a security matter. Direct diplomatic exchanges and 'Track Two' talks are said to have brought both countries close to agreement on all three, including Siachen, but further progress has stalled because Pakistan holds solutions on other issues hostage to significant concessions in respect of Kashmir.

As Indians we are convinced that Pakistan has no case on Kashmir and are at best prepared to consider access to the Valley for citizens of the neighbouring country. Across the LOC, a seventy-five-year-old narrative to the contrary has become embedded deep in the national psyche. To put it very briefly, the Pakistan take on Kashmir is as follows: The Partition Plan called for Muslim majority areas to go to the new country. Jammu and Kashmir was a princely state with a Hindu ruler and a Muslim majority. The same principle as was cited with respect to Junagadh (with a Muslim ruler and a Hindu majority) should have been applicable here. India cheated and arm-twisted an accession deed out of the Raja and sent troops to suppress the local population that had risen in protest. The dispute was raised at the United Nations Security Council, which called for a plebiscite. However, India has refused to countenance such a process though it was the party that first approached the UNSC.

Important facts have been omitted from this narrative, which has been fed to and believed by Pakistanis for all this time. Blurred from the account of the popular uprising are the raising and dispatch by the Pakistan Army of tribal lascars from the Frontier Province. Obscured also is the fact that people from the Valley and adjoining regions turned against these invaders. From talks I had with people from the hill regions, I am convinced that the royal family had loyalists in this area who would have supported Maharaja Hari Singh's decision. In any event, the official account does not outright refute that Sheikh Abdullah was the most popular leader in the Valley though it stays silent on the fact that he was on balance in favour of India. Lastly, the Pakistani public has been kept in the dark about the stipulations that must be fulfilled—including the withdrawal of all troops bar an Indian policing contingent—before conditions can be deemed conducive for a plebiscite.

As a net result of the propagandizing through such half-truths, ordinary Pakistanis had developed a sense of entitlement in regard to Jammu and Kashmir. They did truly believe the statements of their rulers, civilian and military, that the absorption of the State into their nation's territory was 'the unfinished agenda of Partition'. For them, Kashmir was the paradise on earth they were cheated of and its 'recovery' was essential for the nation to develop a sense of itself.

After the insurgency broke out, news outlets began adding on India's troop strength and scale of civilian deaths almost exponentially. On the deployment graphs the figure reached half a million and the casualty count hit 70,000 by the middle of 1990. No sources, independent or otherwise, were ever cited in support of those figures. Distorted presentations of this sort bred moral outrage and genuine anger towards India. Very often, when the 'government-sponsored atrocity' angle was played up, even generally sober-minded Pakistanis would be induced to say, 'Your country has gone too far this time. We should not have anything to do with you people.'

Rage and hatred aroused by the Kashmir issue was further fuelled by what the ordinary citizens heard and read about the treatment of Muslims in India. There were very few allusions, if at all any, to stories of success in business and other fields scored by our country's largest religious minority. The fact that three from the community had been Presidents of India and other individuals had headed the Supreme Court, the Air Force and the national cricket team were skimmed over. It was as if the entire story of the Indian Muslims was about the atrocities committed against them in different localities. There was not the least trace of irony in the spouting of this litany by the members of a nation that treated its own minorities as second-class citizens.

~

While Kashmir and the plight of the Muslims constituted specific grievances, India's totality too seems to be a cause for resentment. Much as we Indians might like to think that this is about envy and a desire to catch up with us, the way this attitude has been shaped has not been so linear. At least up to the early 1990s, it was as much about Pakistanis believing that they were generally better off than us, especially in material terms.

When I went to clear our baggage through customs on first arrival, the staff in Rawalpindi airport had quite a few laughs at my expense. A whole set of keys for the locks on trunks and suitcases could not be found, so with my permission, a handyman was found to do the needful. He used a set of pliers to crack open lock after lock and every snip was greeted with hoots of laughter at shoddy Indian workmanship. Then he opened the shoe box and provided the lady officer in charge with her chance to titter. '*Begum ko kya pehnate hain aap*,' she asked me, pointing to the old sandals that Nandini had not had the heart to leave behind.

By that time, the Maruti revolution had barely hit our streets while any Pakistani with four *murabbas* (one *murabba* is twenty-five acres or *killas*) or more was driving a Japanese-built SUV. (Toyota Land Cruisers replaced Mitsubishi Pajeros as first choice over the three years I was there.) Imported perfumes and accessories were much easier to come by than they were in India and international brands far more common. Given these material conditions, Pakistanis did not seem to appreciate the 'middle class' values that Indians espoused at that time.

Punjab was perhaps richer than many other parts of the subcontinent at the time of Partition. For this reason, probably, the people from the land of the five rivers seem to have been somewhat disdainful of the masses living elsewhere. We have already gone through their martial credentials and there could also have been a streak of the racism of the fair-skinned. Anyone refuting this should remember the treatment given to the people of East Pakistan before the creation of Bangladesh. Then, post-Partition, India seemed to be trapped in the 'Hindu rate of growth'—a term sometimes used to indicate the lower growth rate before the economic reforms of 1991 under P.V. Narasimha Rao—while Pakistan, in unabashed flirtation with the West, was apparently marching to prosperity. It was a situation that would have made them believe they were the upwardly mobile who needed to put distance between themselves and the destitutes who claimed to be their cousins.

At the same time, there were some uncomfortable though irrefutable facts. The 'impoverished masses' on the other side of the Radcliffe Line did manage to integrate a plethora of diverse pieces into one; frame and adopt a constitution; get the British-bequeathed military under civilian control; run a democracy with regular elections; and take significant strides in education, public health, science and technology. Such achievements seemed to get further out of reach as one tinpot after another came forward to control the destiny of the Pakistanis.

It would have been an excruciating experience for the Pakistanis to admit that the 'poverty-stricken *kale log*' have done better in some respects. Awareness of their nation's shortcomings sowed a bitterness against the very establishment that caused this gap to open. In every other season, there would appear articles lamenting the early demise of Jinnah and Liaquat Ali Khan; India's good luck that Nehru lasted until the '60s; and their own military's itch to over-reach. Surprising as it may sound to Indians, there was even anger at the 'Hindu intransigence' that led to Partition and the dumping of the western provinces into the unwholesome embrace of a bloated military.

When I first landed in Pakistan, the ubiquitous presence of STD/ISD booths was the one Indian feature envied by those who had visited. Over time, the transformations visible on our roads, the laying of metro lines in over a dozen cities, the spread of cyber parks and the global impact of IIT and IIM alumni are among the matters that figure prominently in internet commentary. A recent speech by Prime Minister Shehbaz Sharif gives an indication of how the reality and perception of it have both changed. After alluding to the fact that India's IT exports had crossed USD 200 billion, he continued, 'and ours is one billion'. If acceptance in the West is the ultimate criterion for success, Indians have gone beyond visual range. The rest of the world acknowledges that the two countries are no longer on par. Hard data also indicates that India has erased the earlier shortfall in per capita GDP and that our lead is steadily widening.

Just look at our respective cricket teams. Asif Iqbal and his mates were the epitome of style as the 1979–80 series got underway. That Pakistan team had crossed the border to revive cricketing ties after a long gap. When they took the field, wearing Kerry Packer's Channel 9 logo 'Big Boys Play at Night' on their practice T-shirts and oozing the sophistication of county cricket, they set every red-blooded Indian male's teeth on edge. A draw in that series restored balance in the machismo stakes, but till the turn of the millennium, they seemed to shade our boys in glamour.

Today, our team has the better record in general as well as head-to-head match-ups. Both sides also know that the difference is attributable in good part to the vast improvement in Indian infrastructure and that the gap is likely to steadily grow wider. The complete turnaround is obvious off the field as well. Pakistani cricketers look woebegone besides our IPL-enriched millionaires. Imran Khan admitted as much in a speech after his ouster in 2022. In his playing days, the Indian cricketers looked like people who had come from a poor country, he said, before going on to observe that this impression was no longer true.

~

Will the change in the rhetoric emanating from the top echelons of the political class lead to a rethink on attitudes towards India? For the moment, there does not appear to be much of a backlash against the softer rhetoric of the politicians by an unpopular military that has retreated to the barracks. But before jumping to conclusions, it would be useful to remember that Pakistani society is one in which the individual is under multiple pressures to conform.

An incident that took place in Bahrain a few years after my Pakistan assignment comes to mind. It illustrates the way in which conformist societies can easily stop a person from thinking for himself.

Bahrain was my base when I was posted as *The Hindu*'s West Asia correspondent from 1994 to 2002. As a base for covering a beat that stretched from Iran to Morocco and Turkey to Oman, Bahrain was ideal in several ways. However, it had its drawbacks, one of which was that the airport would be closed for a few hours late at night. That invariably meant that I would reach the airport well before it opened whenever I took an early morning flight. So early in fact that the policemen on duty, mostly Pakistanis, would be the only other people around.

On one occasion, a half-dozen of them, who had probably just finished their shift, were sitting in a loose circle sipping tea. One of them was holding forth on a topic the others did not seem familiar with. As he got the more enthused, the seniormost man present seemed to be getting increasingly irritated. Finally, this top cop drawled, '*Woh toh Quran mein bhi likkha hai*.' (It is written in the Quran as well.)

Talk about shut-up calls! The rest together chorused the line about it being written in the Quran. The holder-forth, perhaps a little too emphatically, so as to demonstrate his acquiescence, admitted as much. I do not remember what the topic or the manner of its presentation was, but I am as certain now as I was then that it did not figure in just that way in the holy book.

Senior men all over the world do resort to dirty tricks of this sort when they feel that they are being upstaged by subordinates. One wonders, however, if the surrender would have been as swift and as complete if someone, somewhere else, had said, 'That's written in the Puranas,' or, 'That's written in the Bible,' though cultures across the world certainly appear to be moving in that direction. (India under the current dispensation and the US during the presidency of Donald Trump will serve well enough as Exhibits 'A' and 'B'.) Either way, this was not just about winning an argument. It was as much about reminding the man that hierarchies and official storylines had sanctity. Such spotting and quelling of any sign of independent thinking seemed to me to be an imperative of the culture.

An urge to enforce conformity perhaps emanates from the fear that the nation will lack unity unless everyone subscribes to one set of beliefs. While national integrity is certainly under enormous strain on account of pressure from multiple quarters, factors favouring cohesiveness seem to be unduly overlooked. There are many ingredients that can lead to the natural evolution of a Pakistani sense of identity and of collective value. People in this the western part of the subcontinent can look to their history of the last seventy-five years; their shared experiences; experiments, successful or otherwise, they have undertaken; the intensification of the interactions between themselves; progress made towards integrating their state and society; their hopes for the future; and the awareness that they will have to work collectively to achieve these objectives, probably without support from anyone else.

After all, they have made a beginning in sports. Although no Baloch has made it to the national cricket team as far as I know, it has included Pakhtuns of both tame and wild varieties, Mohajirs, even Hindus and Christians and of course Punjabis from all pockets. Today, when the Men in Green play, there will probably be hardly a household in that country that does not back them. It is a country that can have a sense of unity and common destiny which swings to the tune 'Dil Dil Pakistan' by the group Junoon.

Such a development might not happen so long as the collective mind is not free to breathe. Conformism has to be undermined for this to happen. There is a great deal of frustration at the many hurdles that have been set in place to stifle thinking. This extends to strong resentment against an establishment behind these barriers. As a way of countering these pressures, Pakistanis resort to satire and derisive laughter of which examples have been given in other parts of the book. Several sections in that country have also fought that fight openly and with great courage.

As a print journalist, I like to believe that *Dawn*, one of the world's great newspapers, offers a model. Its pride in its contribution to the Pakistan movement is reflected in its adherence to the values that the founders of the new state promised to uphold. While unstinting in its criticism of India, this newspaper, unlike other outlets would try to ensure that it got the facts straight. It had no reservations about blasting the Guardians or the endless line of charlatans appearing on the national scene either. Liberal, forward-looking and, yes, secular, *Dawn* showed that Pakistan can get its act together.

An interesting attempt to root Pakistan's *astitva* in the territory it occupies was made by Aitzaz Ahsan, Pakistan Peoples Party leader, former federal minister and eminent lawyer. I cannot recall the full details of his thesis, published in a series of articles (and I have not seen the book in which he intended to compile and elaborate on his ideas). From what I remember, his argument was that the land watered by the Indus and its tributaries nurtured an ethos that was distinct from the one that took shape in the Gangetic Plain. The conclusion, if I am not mistaken, was that this Indus ethos could fill out the idea of Pakistan.

While the theory was attractive in its way, it had a fundamental flaw that was identified in a somewhat oblique fashion by the late B.M. Kutty. This Malayali gentleman from Tirur (in the present-day Malappuram district) had been sent to pre-Partition Karachi by the Communist Party to help establish its branches there. He stayed on in the port city after 1947, throwing himself whole-heartedly into the pro-democracy movement, union work and the activities of several NGOs. Mr Kutty's critique of the Ahsan thesis came out in the course of a totally unrelated story that he once narrated to me.

During the endless confabulations between democratic forces that unfolded after the death of Zia and before the 1988 parliamentary election, the participants would apparently seek diversion by talking of less pressing subjects at meal times. One day, during a lunch in Benazir's house, they started chatting about their respective ancestries, about whose forefathers had settled on the land first. The Pirs in the crowd, as Syeds and therefore descendants of the Prophet, had to defer to the Bhuttos, Jatois and Mazaris. These Sindhi feudal clans, presumably Indo-European, had arrived on the scene more than two millennia before. Then Kutty played his trump card.

'None of you are original Sindhis. The ancestors of some of you came from Arabistan, those of others from Persia or Central Asia. I am the only one here who is descended from the original Sindhis because I am Dravidian.'

Although a small group of people speaking a Dravidian tongue—the Brahuis—still survive in Balochistan, I did not come across any. I asked Kutty whether their language was indeed Dravidian-sounding.

'Well,' he said. 'You can find some similarity with Malayalam or Tamil by stretching the imagination. At the same time, it is definitely not Urdu or Hindi.'

Apart from the difficulty Ahsan would have faced in linking present-day Pakistanis to the denizens of Harappa or Moenjodaro, it is unlikely that the putative beneficiaries would be enthused by the discovery. The search for roots does not go so far. A very tall, grossly overweight adherent of the Jiye Sindh moment comes to mind. He had taken me to meet G.M. Syed—mover of the Pakistan Resolution in the Sindh Assembly; later a Sindhi nationalist and founder of the Sindhudesh movement, who spent thirty years of his 92-year life span in jail or house arrest—and while we waited for this doyen of Sindhi independence, then in his eighties or even nineties, to get ready, the portly gentleman filled me in on the features that made Sindhis so unique.

'You remember your Mahabharat don't you? What made

Jayadratta stand out? He was a lover of horses, a lover of beautiful women. That's what we are.'

Perhaps the weaving of a myriad such strands together can lead to the creation of a new national narrative centred on the fact that the Indus basin was a prime site for the melting of cultures that is such a feature of South Asia. As a first step, the people of Pakistan have to look deeper into the history of their land and learn lessons that can be used in future. Before a belief system that originated from West Asia got entrenched in this region, it had a tradition of exporting its own thoughts to other parts of the world. If geography is destiny, a way forward for Pakistan appears to be available. It could be the hub for transit and trade between the billion-plus population of the sub-continent and the countries of West and Central Asia.

The emergence of such a sense of national identity might not lead to the automatic extinguishing of hostility towards India. It will almost certainly not lead to a sense of commonality. That is why Indians who came to Pakistan on week- or fortnight-duration visas—the parachutists as we used to call them—sounded so silly when they assumed that the liberalism they encountered was irrefutable proof that their hosts were ready to forget all differences. Pakistani desire for a liberalized social atmosphere is quite distinct from their feelings about India and the attainment of one need not lead to a change in the other. Those who think otherwise are confusing two matters. Their utterances in this regard sounded as naive as their hosannas to Pakistani hospitality.

Sure, Pakistanis are generally very hospitable. But

they also think that Indians are somewhat lacking in this respect. A very good friend of mine asked me early in our acquaintanceship, 'So, when are you calling me over for a drink.' My reply that I would do so soon became miserably repetitive because the occasion just did not arise. Finally, once, as we were exiting the venue of a press conference he asked, 'Are you calling me home at least today you bloody Bania?' Our friendship was strong enough to withstand my responding with a 'Hypocrite Pakistani can't buy his own booze'.

We two could laugh over our exchange but other Indians and Pakistanis in another set of circumstances might not be able to do so. The banter also points to something deeper. From the Pakistani perspective, 'Indian miserliness' probably constitutes a quality they can never be comfortable with. For us, their assumption of being the ultimate hosts can be just as irritating. There are enough granular differences of this sort that will set us apart as peoples.

Even a 'normal', democratic, Pakistan might well decide that its interests are better promoted through confrontation rather than amity. Or, a political party there might instigate hostility towards us to serve its own purposes. We also need to remember that we have failings, perhaps not so obvious to us, that tend to antagonize others. After all, when Bangladesh, Sri Lanka and Nepal are not willing to look on India as some sort of shining beacon, there is little reason to think that Pakistan will.

Affinities

'Never tell them that we are the same people,' Rajendra Sareen told me when I sought his guidance before taking on the Pakistan assignment. 'If you do, they'll immediately ask you, "Then why did we have Partition?"'

Sareen Saab, founder and head of Public Opinion Trends Analysis and News Service, was in my opinion the foremost among the Indians who sought to study and understand Pakistan. Even till today, more than two decades after his passing, hardly anyone else has come close to matching his insight into the mind of our vexatious neighbour. He was born and came of age there, he spoke and wrote Urdu and Punjabi and he could unerringly trace the ticking of the brain cells on the other side of the border. No sensible person could ignore advice emanating from such a source.

You might not feel the difference when running into a Pakistani in a mixed crowd at a party in the Gulf or other parts of the world outside the subcontinent. After a few weeks in Pakistan you might not feel the difference when you mix with a crowd of fellow professionals in Islamabad. But when you find yourself for the first time among a group made up mostly of Pakistanis, there is an unmistakeable sense that you are in a different milieu. And that sense is awoken not merely by the sight of so many Awami suits around you.

I had felt a similar strangeness when I went for the first time to our Punjab, Kashmir, and even Madhya Pradesh for that matter. Although I had interacted with people from most States while living in Delhi, there is after all a difference when you walk into another's home turf. In Lahore and then Islamabad in the first few days I certainly felt that difference and something more. On looking back so many years later, I am more keenly aware now than I was then that it was not just a matter of missing cues or reading them wrongly.

(Speaking of being on home turf or otherwise, it is a given that on neutral ground everyone is adjusting to others even if unwillingly or unconsciously. When you are in another's home turf, you can feel the pressure of that culture since the local boys are under no compunction to adjust.)

As my ability to read the social terrain picked up, this sense of strangeness did abate somewhat. Differences that were obvious at first glance lost their sharp edges and got pushed into the recesses of the mind. However, the nuances did not fade altogether and with unpleasant incidents cropping up like coral, a mental barrier steadily developed. That did not happen to me in East Punjab or MP, not even in Kashmir. While a level of reserve in dealing with Pakistanis did become palpable, explanations of its nature and causes are tied up with analysis of macro factors and hence best left aside for the moment. For now it is sufficient to say that memories of animosity directed at me and reciprocated remain encrusted in the mind.

When it comes to the pinning down of differences, the task is not so straightforward. Sights, sounds and smells change once you cross the line between the two countries. But such variations occur when you move from State to State or even between districts in India and contrasts can sometimes be drastic. Besides, we South Asians get so accustomed to the processing of diversity almost from birth that a few alterations here and there do not entail strenuous effort.

As the irrepressible Shoaib Hashmi—Economics professor, playwright, theatre actor, son-in-law of Faiz Ahmad Faiz and master of irreverent commentary—once wrote in his column in *Friday Times*, 'We look more or less alike, we speak more or less the same language, we eat more or less the same food, listen to the same music and laugh at the same jokes. But of course we are not the same people.'

Hashmi Saab was lampooning Pakistani officialdom's incessant hammering on the message of dissimilarity. My intent in including his comment here is only to show the difficulty of pinpointing the distinctions that do exist.

It is somewhat akin to having astigmatism of the mental vision. For a moment you are absolutely certain that you have arrived at an accurate conception of the situation in front of you and then, suddenly, 'Whoa! Where did that come from?' It is not an experience that is always unsettling. Sometimes it is exhilarating, at yet other times amusing.

Here I am not talking about encounters with what I would call 'officially-sponsored Pakistanis'. Those experiences can be understood as soon as they begin to unfold and are invariably wearisome in the extreme.

As sought to be brought out in earlier chapters, there has been a conscious effort to contrive an ideal of what a Pakistani—especially male Pakistani—ought to be. Even if such an ideal might have been initially propounded by a non-official ideologue, it appears to have acquired official approval somewhere down the line. So much so that it is almost of the nature of a state-sponsored template. A model that is supposed to amalgamate the values he should strive for and exhibit—a self-image. As has also been seen, these efforts by the Guardians of Ideology have at best met with mixed, or perhaps only, partial success. You do come across people who swagger about with the required Islamic martial fervour. But you will also notice that nearly all other Pakistanis present are looking into the middle distance trying to cover their embarrassment. Although no one will challenge the swaggerer because they assume he has backing, they clearly give the impression that they wish he was far away.

If most Pakistanis have not bought into the officially-sponsored model and are also discernibly not Indians, what are they? This question can be answered by highlighting the stark differences. While that may be the easier option, it might be more interesting to go through a list of commonalities while keeping a keen eye out for the points of departure.

~

At this point, I must beg the indulgence of the reader. From what follows in the passages below, it will be obvious that I am giving vastly undue prominence to my *'jaat bhais'*.

Malayalis make up a microcosm of a minority of the population of Pakistan and are so marginal that most of their compatriots are unaware that they exist. However, I did say that I was going to go through a list of commonalities and what can make for a stronger sense of identity than a language that confines us to the margins in either country?

On my first evening in Karachi, I was invited to dinner by an Indian diplomat. He asked me to meet him at the Consulate since he felt that I might not easily locate his address. The Pakhtun taxi driver was new to the city and while generally familiar with the layout of Clifton, the neighbourhood in which the Consulate was situated, was unable to find the street. We spotted two men striding down the pavement of an otherwise deserted street and pulled up near them to ask for directions. As soon as I heard the accent in which one of them said '*Indian embassiyo?*' I switched to Malayalam. Yes! They were my linguistic brethren and they were only too happy to point the way. But they were wearing Awami and both were burly enough to pass for the taxi driver's kin.

B.M. Kutty did not lose touch with his roots even in the last years of his life and he was ever conscious of his Malabariness. At the end of his first visit to my house he said, 'I never thought that one day in Islamabad I would be given *dosa* for breakfast by a Malayali woman.'

On another occasion he tried to put me in touch with a retired Junior Commissioned Officer of the Pakistan army. On the phone, this gentleman was both cautious and amused. He seemed to be tickled by the idea of speaking to an enemy while sitting in his drawing room. We never met up because the unwritten rules did not permit that but his

Malayalam had so little rust on it that he must have been using it regularly. Since he was a resident of Rawalpindi it surely meant that there were other Malayalis in khaki to provide him company.

Affinities of this sort can cut both ways. There was a story told among South Indians in the Indian High Commission about a Malayali who tried to bypass the bugs on his phone by speaking to someone in his native tongue. According to the narrators, a voice cut into the conversation and told those who were on the line: '*Aiynum ibade aallindu tto.*' (There are people here for that as well.)

In Karachi I almost never bought cigarettes despite being a smoker. Many of the tea shops and kiosks were run by Moplahs who only had to hear my South Malabar Nair accent to wave away payment. If not for the hostility between the two countries, the hospitality would have extended beyond smokes to a chicken biryani at least.

Karachi Malabaris are one of those freaky by-products of history. People who have never lived near the coast of the Arabian Sea seem to have no inkling of the significance of a trade route that flourished from antiquity until the 1960s. In Kozhikode, where I spent my holidays as a child, the waters south of the government-owned wharves would be filled with dhows for most months of the year. The wharves were used to load lighters that carried cargo out to the steamships anchored in deeper water. But the beach south of the wharves was filled with chandler shops and other establishments that serviced the dhows.

Those dhows sailed to a pattern known as the double triangle that was set more than two millennia ago. In the months before the onset of the southwest monsoon, these lantern-rigged wooden sailing vessels would cross the Arabian Sea from Dar-es-Salaam or other ports in East Africa to the Malabar coast. After unloading at the Kerala landfalls, they would sail on up the Konkan to Kutch and then Karachi. From there, with the north-east monsoon behind them, they would cover the last leg of the triangle back to Africa. On the other triangle, the vessels would travel from India to Africa, follow that coast up to the Red Sea, then turn eastward for the Gujarat coast.

If anyone ever extols the virtues of Malabari betel leaf before a true-blue Banarsi *paanwallah* he might well be spat upon. But the broad, dark green leaf grown on the slopes below the ridge line from Valancheri to Kottakkal in Malappuram district was apparently much prized in Karachi. The Moplahs, following their tradition as sea-faring traders, had set up shop in what became Pakistan's commercial capital long before Partition.

For many, Partition spelt the beginning of their problems. All of a sudden, visas, passports and consulate visits had to be inserted into the simple task of travelling to meet their kin. Some ingenious methods have been worked out to get around these problems, especially after the Emirates of the Gulf started providing convenient transit (and passport-switching) points. But I did come across one gentleman who, speaking pure Tirur Malayalam, lamented that he had 'entered like a rat into a trap and got caught'.

Kutchi Memons—a distinction is nowadays drawn between the Sindhi and Kutchi varieties though this is probably superficial—presumably a few notches higher in the financial pecking order, seemed more or less indifferent to the formalities of trans-border travel. Indeed, they seemed to treat Mumbai and Karachi as interchangeable homes. One of them, Sattar Bhai, the greatest foodie I have ever come across (he could even beat my grand-uncle Muthu Achan who was a formidable trencherman) literally put himself at the disposal of Nandini and me. He not only arranged a luncheon meeting with a Chamber of Commerce but took us across to Thatta to eat with his relatives, meet Hindu families and see the strange, elaborate tombs of Sufi saints that sprout alongside the highway between the metropolis and the provincial town.

At that time, I first thought that it was the cosmopolitanism of his community that made him so nonchalant about the risks of mingling so freely with Indians. I later realized that it was actually his utter innocence that made him so free. On every occasion on which we met up after that I felt enormous relief that the various branches of his country's intelligence services seemed to find him as harmless as I did.

Kutchis, Bohras and Parsis gave Karachi an air of freedom that Lahore never seemed to match. That sense of looseness was an illusion. By the early 1990s, the city had been turned into a conglomeration of warring neighbourhoods between which pitched battles often erupted. The Mohajir Qaumi Movement (as it was known before the first word in its name changed from Mohajir—'refugee'—to Muttahida—'united') had established political hegemony over the metropolis. Its armed gangs protected (or terrorized) the neighbourhoods populated by Urdu-speakers from the Gangetic plain who had crossed over in 1947. MQM bands were opposed by the Pakhtun gangs that were supposedly protecting their own neighbourhoods. While the Urdu-speakers made for the larger numbers, the Pakhtuns could call on the well-armed fighters who were on rest and recreation breaks from the Afghan war.

Although I visited a number of Mohajir strongholds in the course of about a half dozen visits to Karachi, I never came remotely close to a gunfight. Nor did I ever visit any Pakhtun neighbourhood since it would have been suicidal for an Indian to venture into the backyard of Mujahideen zealots, even those on furlough. With the terms of my visa specifically stipulating that I was not to meet Afghan refugees or go anywhere near their camps, any such venture would have also probably led to an early forced exit from the country. There was no way of convincing myself that the story to be gained through a heroic foray was worth the risk. At some point down the years, Daniel Pearl concluded otherwise and despite the tragic outcome his choice needs to be honoured.

My experiences were of an almost surreal nature in the Mohajir neighbourhoods. Streets in those parts were usually gated or had barricades thrown across them. According to rumours, these barriers were backed up by bastions in the houses nearby. As soon as the taxi came to a halt at the gates, its doors would be flung open by young men who looked like the cousins of my Bihari friends from college.

No one ever brandished a weapon in my face, perhaps because they did not need to. Outlines of pistol butts at waistbands and telltale bulges under other parts of clothing provided sufficient indication. Second-hand knowledge about the state of affairs prepared the visitor to deal with the unmistakable trace of menace. What was more likely to throw him off balance was the chaste Urdu, coasting on a Purbiya cadence, with which he would be asked to state his business.

In those days Mohajirs would claim that they could easily identify an outsider from that person's inability to correctly pronounce the Urdu alphabet 'Qaf'. That usually meant a Punjabi, Sindhi or Pathan. The Malayali could not come anywhere close to a correct pronunciation either but since the rest of his words were equally off-key it did not really matter. Apart from the Bhojpuri lilt, another comforting factor was the MQM's reputation for being relatively secular. It did not mean that there were any non-Muslims in its hierarchy or that its leaders were not devout. It did, however, mean that my own religious label never caused a problem for me in Mohajir country.

Here again, readings of the situation should not go too far in the other direction. My friend Javed Ansari, then with *India Today*, visited Karachi around that time to meet long-separated relatives. An India–Pakistan cricket match happened to take place somewhere in the world around that time (possibly the clash in Australia during the '92 World Cup). As Javed was to write later in his magazine, his cousins praying fervently during each over would at the breaks tell their Indian visitor that Allah was sure to grant them victory. Javed wrote that he was aghast to hear himself retort, 'India will win if Allah has anything to do with it since there are more Muslims on that side than on this.'

The MQM was to offer another parallel with India, albeit

one re-aligned by time. Its leader, Altaf Hussain, was the pioneer of the marathon political monologues that became a feature in a very distant part of India. Long before J. Jayalalitha took up the practice, Hussain had got into the habit of speaking non-stop for hours. At first it was through personal appearances at venues in Karachi. Later, after he had removed himself to London when his own town became too dangerous, it was by video-conference.

At the time I was in Pakistan, the MQM problem seemed intractable. Hussain was going all out to demarcate and consolidate his power base in the towns of Sindh province where the '47 refugees had mainly settled. This put the MQM at loggerheads with both Sindhi feudals, who were unwilling to share power in their ancestral land, and Pakhtuns who had their own pockets in the towns. Most Sindhi feudals were grouped in the PPP but a number of them had quit the party when Benazir was ousted from the premiership in 1990. Led by a real character called Jam Sadiq Ali, the dissident Sindhis had formed coalitions with the Muslim League and the MQM in the Centre and the province.

These three disparate forces, with barely concealed support from the military, were on an all-out campaign to finish the PPP. While the League had little muscle in the province, the MQM had it in spades and the party made full use of the licence given to it by Chief Minister Jam Sadiq Ali and the military. For the two years plus that he ran the provincial government, Jam Saheb was able to keep the balance between his own supporters and the MQM with his right hand and keep the federal government at bay with the other. After his time, Altaf Hussain and the MQM became near uncontrollable.

That the army was then headed by a Mohajir, Mirza Aslam Beg, probably had something to do with the freedom to operate initially granted to the party. This nexus with the military was to break down probably because of the MQM's own intransigence, and the next Mohajir to head the army, Pervez Musharraf, authorized the body blows from which the party does not seem to have recovered.

~

Away from the bristling neighbourhoods, Karachi could be really urbane. On entering the panelled halls of the Sindh Club, with the heads of long-dead animals mounted on the walls, it took no stretch of the imagination to believe that one had been transported to its sister institutions in Bengaluru or Secunderabad. The food too, if I remember correctly, was no different—an outstanding dish or two backed by the same sort of mutton curry and caramel custard churned out by Club *khansamas* throughout the subcontinent as if they had all been trained in the same culinary school.

(The Karachi Press Club had opted for the more sensible route of hiring cooks who could turn out proper Awadhi fare with melting *kababs* and *rotis* that turned to vapour in the mouth. It was a really lively place and I assert as much even though I never got to go there for an evening. After sunset, the rooms on its first floor apparently became enclaves independent of the restraints applicable to the rest of the Islamic Republic.)

There was a surprise for me on my first visit to the Sindh Club. I had been invited for lunch by the former army officer and then renowned columnist M.H. Askari. It was our first face-to-face encounter and after the greetings Askari Saab stumped me by asking, 'How is Babychechi?'

Very few outside a tight circle in Thrissur would have known that Babychechi was the affectionate name for Dr Vimala Nair, a leading gynaecologist in her time. Before I fully recovered from the shock of hearing her name being mentioned aloud in the Sindh Club, Askari said that he had served under her husband Colonel Kesavan Unni Nair on the Burma Front during the Second World War. The conversation flowed freely and fast during that lunch and it was only years later—quite recently actually—that I bothered to try and unravel the puzzle.

There was never any reason to doubt that Askari had served under Col Unni Nair. But how had he known that I knew Dr Vimala? In point of fact, I knew her very well since she was our next door neighbour for almost a decade. Still, other than the *jaati*-network connection, which is very strong, there was no obvious link between me and her. Askari had either made a stupendously shrewd guess or some friend in the intelligence services had provided him with a dossier on me that was far more detailed than I had ever imagined.

One of my favourite stories concerns my father-in-law, Lt Col (retd.) M. Sathesan of the Corps of Signals, Indian Army. Actually, it was one of my favourites until I got so tired by the repetitions that I invariably head for the door whenever he launches into it. For all that, it is a very interesting story, definitely worth recounting.

My father-in-law had studied in the Madras Christian

College High School in the 1930s. In school he had two good friends, the brothers Saleem and Kaleem, who were the grandsons or nephews of a judge. On Partition, this family shifted to Pakistan and all contact was lost. Soon after I told Nandini's father about our posting to Pakistan he salvaged an old school photograph, which had the images of himself and his two friends and charged me with the task of tracking them down. I made the usual accommodating noises but secretly resolved that I was going to leave for the good Colonel's daughter the very exciting task of finding two needles in a few million haystacks.

My wife is a very determined woman and a very faithful daughter. Once she had finished the business of setting up home, she embarked on her mission. She found an immediate ally in Mrs Uma Sreedharan, wife of the naval attaché in the Indian High Commission, Captain Arjun. Uma was heading for a party at the house of a lady who had a remote Chennai connection and promised to show the photo. We got her call at about the time the party should have started. She had shown the snap to the mother of the hostess, who had taken one look at it and exclaimed, '*Yeh toh mere bete hain.*' (These are my sons.)

The old dowager was an unreconstructed, sari-clad Madrasi. I cannot recall whether she could speak Tamil. Perhaps not since they were always Urdu speakers at home, but she could pronounce South Indian names without a vowel misplaced. I remember her speaking of an old acquaintance, Vishwanatha Menon, with the correctly elongated 'eh' in the middle of the first syllable of the surname and 'awn' of the second. Saleem had migrated to the United Kingdom and

Kaleem was in Karachi so the good Colonel did not meet them when he came to Pakistan. But his daughter and her mystified husband did, without ever getting over the buzz at the surprise.

There is a flip side to the story. The son-in-law of the Chennai dowager, in whose house the drama had first unfolded, ran a business that catered to the needs of the diplomatic missions. Business enterprises of the sort are probably ubiquitous in all capital cities. They were indispensable in a town like Islamabad, which was a bureaucratic enclave with a cosmetic screen of commercial zones. Rawalpindi, so close that it was virtually a Siamese twin, was not much more than a jumped-up cantonment town on the lines of Dehradun.

All the stuff needed to make embassy offices and staff housing serviceable and ritzy had to be trucked up from Karachi. No one running a business that serviced the missions could have done so without the approval of the intelligence services. It does not take a genius to figure out that such approval would not be granted unless the businessman in question did a lot of work for the back room boys or was one of them.

Border-transcending connections are of course far more common in Karachi and other places where migrants from India settled. But they are not exactly non-existent in those parts of Pakistan from where a goodly portion of the once-native population was driven out in '47. One of the High Commission's senior officers, whose stint more or less overlapped with mine, got in touch with his father's sister. The family came from Kohat in the Frontier and she had stayed back with her Muslim husband when her parents and siblings went away. The officer's father came to Pakistan during that time and she, accompanied by her very gracious husband, met up with her brother after a gap of more than forty years.

~

The connections were not necessarily emotion-laden. They could sometimes be downright incongruous. My driving license had expired before I left Delhi but the relevant authorities on the other side went through the process of granting me a learner's and then the regular license in double-quick time. Then it was Nandini's turn. The SHO of the closest Pindi police station, with whom I had a bantering acquaintanceship, had assured me that the process would be a mere formality if Nandini had a valid Indian license. We went over with the document issued by the Motor Vehicles Department in Tamil Nadu's Pollachi and handed it to the SHO.

'*Yeh toh bilkul hamare jaisa hai,*' was the instant comment of the startled Pakistani. (This is just like ours.) It indeed was, from the exactly matching dimension of the palm-sized booklet to the thin red cloth of the cover peeling at the edges. Even the entries inside followed much the same order except that one was in Tamil and the other would be in Urdu.

In uncharitable moments I could think of a more cynical reason for this solicitousness in the grant of driving licenses. It made the task of my 'followers' a little easier if I was driving around since the usually two-man surveillance teams would then only need to follow the vehicle. If I did not have my own wheels, one of them would have needed to follow on foot while the other shuttled from point to point until I got hold of a taxi.

At the time of the 1993 parliamentary election, the Pakistan Muslim League had split, with one faction headed by Hamid Nasir Chattha crossing over to the Peoples Party's side. On a visit to Chattha's house, a little off the highway, I took note of two little details. The first was that the *shalwar* and *kameez* of the Awami seemed to be clothes reserved for more public places. Off the highway, the Punjabi peasant evidently preferred *lungis* and *banians* much like his counterparts east of the border.

The second feature noticed was that banners and posters strung in the little markets along the highway were different from those along the farm roads. Chattha was not at home—a rural *kothi* with straw strewn on the drawing room floor between mismatched heavy furniture—so I passed on my observation to one of his senior advisers. It seemed as though the markets wanted Nawaz Sharif while the farmlands tilted towards Chattha, I told the man. He did a double-take and then remarked, 'Yes! It is much the same as it is in your country.'

When I met the same person several days later, he told me that he had passed on my observation to Chattha, and that his leader, in a speech, had taken it on by telling his supporters that they were the party of the '*Kashgar*' while Sharif's party was that of the '*Sahukar*'. At that time, the Sharif family was still identified with its Ittefaq Group of industries even though it had bought much farmland to add feudal swagger in a country where *zamindars* counted for more than the commercial classes.

An obverse of this story was narrated to me by Salamat Ali, the veteran journalist who based himself in Delhi after defying the Zia dictatorship (he was jailed during that time). He wrote for the *Far Eastern Economic Review* and was such a fixture in the Lutyens' city journalistic circles that I did not even know he was a Pakistani until he returned to his own country. During his stint in India, this Ambala-born gentleman became close to several Indian politicians, especially Chaudhary Charan Singh.

Chaudhary Saab would often ask Salamat Ali to accompany him on the campaign trail. On the first occasion, Ali ventured to point out that there might be visa restrictions since he was a foreigner. '*Tu kaunsa firang ho?*' was the blunt retort from that last undisputed patriarch of the Jat community. (How are you a foreigner?)

Salamat Ali told me another story that stayed with me because it was a match to one that I could narrate a little later. His account concerned J.N. Dixit, that nuclear-powered dynamo of a man who had already done much two-thirds of the way into his professional life and was to do more. Dixit Saab was Joint Secretary, External Publicity, at the time when Salamat was in Delhi and a regular participant in the 4 pm Shastri Bhawan briefings. The Pakistani journalist noticed that Dixit always seemed to have more time for him than for the rest of the foreign correspondents. Perplexed, he asked for an explanation.

'You see,' said Dixit, 'with you I can jump from A to F

and then to Z, knowing that you'll be able to fill the stuff in between. With those *goras* and others I have to go from A to B to C and so on. It's too bloody tiring.'

My story lacks a similar punchline and it is also self-serving. It still brings out one of the irrefutable facts about the Indo-Pak interaction—the relative ease with which we can read each other.

At the end of the first year of my stint, I was flying back to Delhi for what my bosses graciously acknowledged was a 'much deserved' break. From my seat in economy, I could see Pakistan's then Foreign Secretary Shahryar Khan and High Commissioner Abdus Sattar filing into the business section of the Pakistan International Airlines plane. They were headed for a round of Foreign Secretary-level talks, and though I had no professional duties in connection with it, I asked the cabin crew for permission to go across and pay my respects.

Sattar had never set eyes on me before so the expression of appreciation on his face when Shahryar introduced me could not have been feigned. 'I must congratulate you on some first-class political reporting from Pakistan,' he said. 'It's your reports I rely on to find out what's going on in my country.' A couple of years later, when the fight between the President and Prime Minister of Pakistan was at its peak, Shahryar Saab was to tell me that he would wait for the cuttings of my reports so that he could follow the story.

~

A sense of this affinity was not absent even within the holy precincts of the establishment. Captain Anil Bakshi, who had replaced Arjun as our naval attaché, was told about a high-seas encounter by a Pakistani admiral. This admiral was apparently commanding a flotilla that came face-to-face with an Indian frigate. The captain of the Pakistani ship ordered the battening of hatches and set his vessel on a collision course. At the same moment, the Indian captain also sent his ship charging down the same sea-lane.

Such games of chicken are apparently not unknown and there is a protocol to it. Both ships turn 'hard to port' before they smash into each other and the point of the exercise is to find out who holds his nerve longer. On this particular occasion a lieutenant on the flag deck apparently turned to the Admiral and asked whether his captain had not done splendidly. The Admiral's reply, as narrated to Anil, was, 'So did the Indian.'

Anil also had a conversation with Lt Gen Asad Durrani that touched on the peculiar equation between the two countries. Durrani, who was to head both the ISI and Military Intelligence in the course of his career, was serving in a unit that had captured some Indian soldiers in a battle of the 1971 war and was questioning them. He noticed a Sikh among the lot and beckoned him over.

'*Oye Sardara,*' Durrani said he told the man, '*Kaunsa fauji changa? Indian ya Pakistani?*' (Hey Sardar! Who is the better soldier? Indian or Pakistani?)

'*Dono change hain ji,*' our jawan was said to have replied. '*Jiska dhaak chale, wohi Sikander.*' (Both are equally good. Whoever's trick works becomes the conqueror.) Durrani claimed that he found the reply so appropriate that he let the man off interrogation.

An exchange I had with an inspector-level officer of Pakistan's Intelligence Bureau cut even closer to the bone. Although we did not get deeply into the matter for obvious reasons, he seemed to have a supervisory role over the detail assigned to keep watch on the Indian journalists. He was into his middle-age, carried himself with authority, and came around only a couple or three times a week.

One evening during my last month in Pakistan we bumped into each other just outside the Covered Market near the Embassy Road. He invited me to join him for a cup of tea in the nearby stall outside. I declined at first because I was in a hurry but changed my mind when he went on, '*Aap toh hamare saath chai nahi piyenge kyonki aapka dost joh hai na, Kapoor Saab, woh toh bada sakht hai. Aakhir woh saab hain toh hamare department ke.*' (You won't have a cup of tea with us because of your friend Kapoor Saab. He's very tough. After all, he's from our department.)

My friend was indeed head of security for the High Commission and a very tough officer. But I knew that he would not mind if I had a chat over a cup of tea and so sauntered over to the kiosk. Just then the Indian High Commission bus, filled with staff returning home after the day's shift, turned into the road and the exclamation burst from me, '*Hut saala! Ab mera report kal udhar bhi pahonchega.*' (Damn it! Now a report about me will reach there as well tomorrow.)

The Pakistani had not noticed the bus and he turned to me in bewilderment when he heard the words. Then he saw the bus, got my meaning and burst into uproarious laughter.

~

On that Swat Valley trip I have written about earlier, we had reached the Tourist Department guesthouse in a place called Bahrain after a long drive and were hoping to rest after lunch. Sleep became impossible because the children of a holidaying family playing in the lawn would yell at regular intervals: 'Ready, steady, apple, go'. (Why bring in the apple, I never found out.)

Instead of lounging about in the room, we decided to go for a walk down the long sloping road from the guesthouse to the river bed below and met the fathers of our tormentors on the way. They were middle-level corporate executives from Lahore and, as is usual in Pakistan, welcomed us to their country but with more dignified reserve than the norm. They made a few polite enquiries about conditions in India and then walked off perhaps not wanting to spoil their holiday.

They were not rude or aloof and they smiled when they saw us in the dining room. Their reserve could have stemmed from worry that they could get into trouble if seen to be friendly with Indians. There also could have been something more. It is entirely possible that they were the exact counterparts of the Indians who would ask us, 'What's it like over there?' They too seemed to be conveying the message—'We do want to know what life is like in your country though, mind you, we have no intention of visiting that place.'

There was one occasion on which a few people strongly expressed nostalgia for places in India even when it was plain that they were most unlikely to visit. In the summer of 1993, the Organization of the Islamic Conference Foreign

Ministers meeting was held in Karachi. Of the five Indian correspondents in Pakistan, three of us, Vinod Sharma (*Hindustan Times*), Sujit Chatterjee (*PTI*) and I went to cover it while Sunil Narula (*Times of India*) and Suresh Chopra (*AIR*) did not.

For three days, life followed the same dreary pattern of endless waits at the venue for sporadic briefings, going to the Central Telegraph Office, preparing and sending the reports through telex. The CTO would be a beehive in the evenings with staff and journalists jostling about, careful not to trip over the feet of policemen keeping a watch on the goings-on.

The conference ended on a Thursday and Vinod and Sujit left. I went to the CTO late on Friday afternoon to give the staff enough time to reassemble after Jumma prayers and help me send a last report. The place was pleasantly quiet with few staffers, and even more pleasurably, no policemen. I typed the report, punched the tape and threaded it onto the machine for dispatch, helped by a member of the staff. Then the rest drifted closer.

Two of them belonged to families that had migrated from Karwar and the third traced his roots to Ratnagiri. They wanted to know what I could tell them about their 'hometowns'. Unfortunately, I could not tell them much about either place but I had a question for them. They were born in Pakistan, were then in their thirties or forties and their nostalgia for places their parents might have talked about but which they had not seen seemed inexplicable.

'*Aakhir, apna shehr apna hi shehr hai na,*' was the answer. (In the end, one's town is after all one's town.) However, a caveat is very much in order here.

Many Mohajirs had and still have relatives on this side of the border and visits back and forth have familiarized them to quite an extent with conditions in India. They had reason to know, arguably still do, that matters were not as bad as their own media depicted. Some, such as Agha Murtaza Pooya, even flaunted their origins in their own little ways. Pooya, whose family had moved from Madras, wanted to highlight that connection. So when he started a paper he called it *The Muslim* in a gesture of reverse-respect to the Grand Old Lady of Anna Salai—*The Hindu.*

Those gentlemen in the CTO had no intention of going back and resettling in Karwar or Ratnagiri. Their wives and children and presumably whole broods of relatives were in Pakistan. They had good government jobs and were happy enough where they were. Nostalgia for them was just that, a longing that might or might not be fulfilled. They could see very clearly that Partition marked a finality. The thread of a common existence had been severed at that point in time and it was never going to be spliced back again.

Nostalgia's limit was evident from the fact that I never heard a Mohajir, not a single one, ever express a desire to resettle in his original home or wish away the fact of Partition. The Sindhis, Baloch and Pakhtuns appeared close to that point of accepting their status as Pakistanis and the Punjabis had attained certitude on the matter long before.

Differences

'*Kya haal hai, Mussalman, sab theek-thaak?*' (How are you, Mussalman? All well?)

Mahmood Khan Achakzai had given me that moniker when I introduced myself to him as the correspondent of *The Hindu*. But this was probably the first occasion on which he used that particular greeting when we were both within a crowd of Pakistani journalists. Achakzai and the media people were sitting at a table in the canteen of the National Assembly and I had just walked in. On hearing him, my friend Hashmi of *The Muslim* turned to me and said, 'Why don't you call him Hindu and balance the account?'

'Because he's got bodyguards and I don't,' I replied.

After the laughter died down, Achakzai went into an elaboration. 'If they call us Hindu we all go red in the face with anger. They don't get so worked up.' Dry chuckles all round.

Achakzai grinned at me though I thought I saw a trace of sympathy in his eyes. This burly, bald Member of the National Assembly from northern Balochistan was an archetypal Pakhtun in shape, accent and political outlook.

His race had lost its pre-Islamic memories a long, long time ago and they did not seem to be as defensive about those roots as some Punjabis were (perhaps still chafing at the thought that some not-too-distant ancestor had been an infidel). Together with Khan Abdul Wali Khan and Ajmal Khattak, Achakzai was a remnant of the strand of Pakhtun nationalism that had leaned towards the Indian National Congress pre-1947.

Wali Khan, son of the Frontier Gandhi, Khan Abdul Ghaffar Khan, and Ajmal Khattak, who became a Congress activist in the Quit India movement at the age of seventeen, belonged to the Awami National Party. This party had once stood for the merger of the Frontier Province with Afghanistan but had ostensibly settled for the lesser objective of provincial autonomy by the 1990s. Achakzai came from another lineage of ethnic nationalists who had their stronghold in the Pakhtun belt of Balochistan. He represented the Pakhtunkhwa Milli Awami Party in the National Assembly.

Some idea of what Pakhtun nationalists thought of the change in their circumstances since 1947 and the adjustments they had to make is provided by a fairly well-known quote by Wali Khan: 'My family have been Pakhtuns for five thousand years, Muslims for about 1,400 and Pakistanis for a little over forty.' His son Afsandyar Wali continues in the same tradition.

Despite their Pakhtun doughtiness there was an aura about them that suggested a despair that they represented a lost cause. As the 1990s began, Kabul appeared to be on the verge of falling to the Mujahideen, and it did fall in

1992, albeit not to the holy warriors that Pakistan favoured. That took another four or five years to accomplish and it came in the form of the Taliban. At the time I lived in Islamabad, the Pakhtun nationalists on the east of the Durand Line were looking across it with much concern and even more vexation. As far as they were concerned their hopes of keeping Afghanistan on the path of reason and progress depended on the survival of the Najibullah regime. One of their ilk once berated me for India's Afghanistan policy.

'The Afghans were your friends and you completely messed up on the Soviet invasion. Now look at what has happened! These Punjabi bastards are about to get away with everything.'

By then, Baloch nationalism had been reduced to the sadly isolated figure of Bizen Bizenjo. In Sindh, G.M. Syed was just as lonely and an even frailer, older man. The Punjabis, their illegitimacy or otherwise notwithstanding, seemed poised to get away with it all. More so since separatist sentiment in Kashmir had flared up to such levels as to pump up Pakistani expectations that the 'unfinished business of Partition' would soon be concluded to their satisfaction. Almost naturally, this had led to a re-manifestation of a state of mind teetering on the line between vindication and vindictiveness.

Article after article appeared in the print media expounding on the ways in which the surging Islamic fervour would push 'Indian occupation forces' out of Kashmir. The more fervid speculated on how this religion-inspired flood would sweep down to the southern tip of the subcontinent. Newspapers, electronic media, think-tanks and a horde of orators seemed to be vying with each other in escalating the numbers of both 'occupation forces' and victims.

Almost every facet of India was ripped to shreds and degraded. Our military was a bunch of depraved cowards who could resort to all forms of cruelty; our political leaders were cunning, treacherous knaves; our women licentious and our men debased. Our economy was a shambles, our factories churned out shoddy products and more than half our people were starving. Nehru had contrived the horrors of Partition by jumping into bed with Lady Mountbatten, the Mahatma was only a wily Bania not to be compared with the principled Jinnah, so on and so forth. According to these pundits, our sins were about to catch up with us and India was doomed.

The blast of triumphalism waxed at full pitch by the beginning of the 1990s. It did not help that India was then in political turmoil with the Mandal–'Kamandal' confrontations barely subsiding before Rajiv Gandhi was assassinated and a seemingly lacklustre Narasimha Rao took over. The Babri Masjid demolition gave a fillip to the demonization drive when it seemed to be flagging and it never abated fully during the time I stayed in the Islamic Republic.

To bolster their belief that the Almighty would ensure the victory of Virtue over Vice, the Pakistanis had to look no further than the quality of their cricket team of the time. Azharuddin and his boys dutifully followed the World Cup prescription and thrashed the Men In Green in their match-up Down Under, overcoming Javed Miandad's aping (literally) of Kiran More in the process. But Pakistan still lifted the trophy. With Miandad and a young Inzamam-ul-

Haq holding up the batting and the pace trio of Imran Khan, Wasim Akram and Waqar Younis at their most lethal, it was a period when their teams looked more balanced and potent than ours.

For a long period beginning in the second half of the 1980s, Indian fans dared breathe freely only after the last ball. Miandad's six off Chetan Sharma in the 1986 Austro-Asia Cup inflicted a trauma that lasted a long time. Those annual tournaments in Sharjah went so regularly one-way that most Indian fans must have wondered why we bothered to participate. The trauma probably ended only when Misbah-ul-Haq guided the cherry into Sreesanth's hands in the final of the first T20 World Cup in 2007.

While we Indians living in Pakistan had reason to believe that we were the targets of a barrage of hatred and scorn, our tormentors or those encouraging them were not immune from attack. Dissidents had not departed from the scene. Writers who lampooned the holy warriors—Ayaz Amir, then a columnist in *Dawn*, being foremost among them—went at their jobs hammer and tongs. However, they could not match the cacophony from the other side.

It was hay-making time for the '*lifafas*'. In those pre-digital-banking days, payments made to henchmen—by the establishment to sold-out journalists in this case—were delivered in paper envelopes. Thereby the term for the mode of payment became the derogatory handle for the recipients. Seeded throughout the press corps the *lifafas* served as a chorus team for the officially sponsored storyline. A few examples can be given to illustrate their modus operandi.

At a press conference, a minister is prating about the

gratitude expressed by some of the Gulf countries for Pakistan's support during the first Gulf War. For some inexplicable reason he prefers delicacy when stating that the Emirates derided the lack of empathy from 'some other countries'. Even a child who had strayed into that room would have understood which country the honourable minister was alluding to. No matter! A *lifafa* was on hand to do the needful, proclaiming 'India' in a loud voice. He then leaned back in his chair as though it was the corner stool of a boxing ring and he had just knocked down Muhammed Ali.

The disgust that the professional Pakistani journalists felt at this open display of boot-licking was visceral, though none of them said anything. What is the point in arguing with a buffalo?

Illustration Two: A group of journalists are idling away time in a corridor of the National Assembly between sessions. The talk drifts towards the economy and comments are being tossed about desultorily. Then a *lifafa* notices me on the fringes and gets itchy.

'*Suna hai ki India ki economy…*' (I hear that India's economy…), and he makes a swooping downward gesture to finish his sentence and make his point. Marianna Babar, as gutsy a scribe as any to be found in any media culture, shoots the *lifafa* a look of withering scorn and suggests that he find himself a fresher news peg. (Marianna was one of the leading political reporters at that time. She was with *The Nation*, if I remember right, though Pakistani journalists, in the same manner as their Indian counterparts, do switch between papers from time to time.)

Illustration Three was presented in a TV debate about the

attitudes of labour forces. When the talk was thrown open for participation by the audience, one person spoke about the distinctions in attitudes that working men from different countries brought to their jobs. From his experience in the Gulf, he said, the Filipinos were ideal workers. They came to work with full kit and went about their tasks in most business-like fashion. Pakistani workers did their assigned tasks and then lounged around taking no further initiative. That was not very good but still better than people from other countries who had to be driven from their frequent *beedi* breaks. The debate participant did not assign any national label to the third category. That was supplied by the anchor.

'Jaise ki Indians?' (Like Indians?)

Much satisfied laughter from the audience.

The passage of time provided me with sweet revenge. When I was preparing to leave Bahrain a decade later, the packing company sent a team consisting of six Filipinos and one Pakistani. The Filipinos went about their tasks like flesh and blood robots, taking breaks only at prescribed intervals for prescribed periods. Their team's Pakistani man kept going off for what he said were prayers though the great frequency suggested that he had his own notions about religious commandments. Without deviating a whit from their R2D2 imitations, the Filipinos became very animated, laughing and joking about the Pakistani's work habits.

Finally, our man from the Islamic Republic had enough of it. He complained to me bitterly that 'these *Chinis*' were making fun of his religion. His appeal for sympathy went nowhere and he would have been even more embittered if he could have heard the laughter welling within me as the episode brought back the memory of that debate long past.

~

India-baiting fervour was at a very high pitch when I went to introduce myself to a freshly appointed spokesman of the Muslim League. He had such a short stint in the post and thereafter so faded from the scene that I have completely forgotten his name. I do remember that he was a very tall Punjabi with broad shoulders and a craggy face. When I walked into his room, at what was then a very modest party office, he was sitting on a chair behind a modest-sized table, glowering at a paper in front of him. After I responded to his brusque gesture to take a seat, I happened to see that it was a page from an atlas.

'I am trying to find the shortest route to Delhi,' he growled at me. 'I want to get to the Red Fort to raise our flag on its ramparts.'

'Why do you think I am here?' I shot back. 'I want to find the shortest route to the Khyber Pass so that I can raise the Tricolour on the peaks nearby.'

He bellowed in laughter and we struck up a friendship that was all too brief. He dropped by at my house for a cup of tea a few days later. We were both innocent of the ways of Islamabad at that time and did not know that such an exchange was verboten. There might have been other reasons for him losing his job but I think that visit had at least something to do with it.

Months later I asked Husain Haqqani—journalist, academic, diplomat—who acted as a sort of super-spokesman for Prime Minister Nawaz Sharif (and was to ascend to much dizzier heights over the next three decades) whether the removal of the other man was in any way connected to that *chai pe charcha.*

'Maybe he was removed because he took your bootlegger's number,' Haqqani replied with a wicked grin. A Leaguer procuring illicit booze, through an Indian contact to boot, had either committed a grave sin or given his detractors a handy weapon. There were a number of ways by which the official mind could keep tabs on errant behaviour so that the official hand could put an end to it. (I talk about some of my own experiences in the chapter on 'Encrusting Enmity' below.)

Often enough, the itch to demonstrate India's perfidy could be so overpowering that priorities could be turned upside down. In 1991, if my memory serves correctly, there were floods in a large swathe of Punjab and Sindh. It was a time when the whole national effort should have been focused on flood relief and rehabilitation. But, no. Jingoists immediately got on the podium to declare that the inundation had occurred because India had released waters from the eastern tributaries of the Indus without warning. After a briefing by the minister concerned, at which the accusation had not been repeated, I asked the gentleman in private whether the warning had been issued as it should have been under the terms of the Indus Waters Treaty.

The minister, a feudal from one of the central districts of Punjab who was known to be quite a hardliner on India, smiled as he shook his head. 'Don't go by all that gossip. The warnings came well in time as per the terms of the Treaty.'

There was a time when the Kashmiri separatist Amanullah Khan launched a series of marches to the LOC threatening unarmed breaching of the border fence. Khan, a fretful man in those days, was perhaps trying to assert his continued relevance when fresher faces had appeared on the scene. Whatever his motives, he did manage to create impressions of looming crises on each of these occasions. His efforts certainly gave cause for much coded telegraphic messaging between the High Commission and the Ministry of External Affairs and for some anxiety among us Indian reporters. While the threats progressively leaked force on subsequent occasions, uncertainty ran high prior to the first march.

At a Foreign Office briefing, the official spokesman ducked and weaved in the course of avoiding a direct answer to the question of what the Pakistani authorities would do when Khan and his crowd reached the border at Chakothi. He finally fobbed us off with the abstruse comment that his government would fulfil its obligations under the Shimla Agreement. This was an accord signed by Indira Gandhi and Zulfiqar Ali Bhutto in Shimla in 1972 that led to the release of 93,000 Pakistani soldiers captured in Bangladesh in the 1971 war and the establishment of the Line of Control. It was hoped that the two sides would use it as a platform to resolve all their differences, which of course has not happened. I managed to chase the gentleman down before he entered the lift and asked him what his comment meant precisely.

'It means that we will stop them,' he replied flat out, his

tone neither defensive nor jocular. Talk about being deflated. All that sound and fury literally signifying nothing.

At other times, reminders of the antagonistic relationship could come in the form of a jiu-jitsu throw. The terrace cafeteria in the Islamabad office of *The Muslim* was a great place for tea, snacks and free-wheeling conversation. One evening, the talk was mainly about the meanderings of a former bigwig in the US State Department. The lady in question was no longer in office, though that fact could have been missed given the attention she was given first in Islamabad and afterwards in New Delhi.

'Yah! She's being exhibited all over the place like a captured Patton tank,' I exclaimed only for my friend Hussein to retort immediately and with some force, 'You mean like a captured Centurion.'

(For those unclear as to the point of our exchange, in the 1965 war, the Pakistani army made a major thrust in the Khemkaran Sector with state-of-the art Patton tanks. Our forces had to match it with British-origin Centurion tanks of an older vintage. After the war, each country shipped armoured vehicles captured from the other to different parts of their respective territories and put them on display.)

On at least one occasion, the playing out of the theme produced a haunting sadness. In an article, a retired senior Pakistan Army officer suggested that the Battle of Basantar (one of the crucial confrontations of the 1971 war) had been a waste of time and effort. He was countered by another of equal rank and seniority who wrote of the heroism displayed by the tank men who fought in that clash. It was of course natural that he wrote about Sowar Muhammad Hussain

Janjua who had won the Nishan-e-Haider for his part in the battle. What came as a surprise was that he went on to pay a glowing tribute to Second Lieutenant Arun Khetarpal of Poona Horse who won the Param Vir Chakra for taking on four enemy tanks single-handedly.

'I refuse to believe,' the gentleman wrote, 'that these two supremely brave young men threw away their lives for nothing.'

~

There were times when the sustaining of the nothing-in-common theme bordered on the farcical. I studiously attended and extensively covered two court cases during my tenure. One involved General (retd.) Mirza Aslam Beg, who relinquished the office of Chief of Army Staff only about a year before he was made the respondent in a case before a Rawalpindi court. The second was the writ petition brought by Nawaz Sharif in 1993 against his dismissal from prime ministership by the then President Ghulam Ishaq Khan.

Lawyers appearing on either side in both the cases seemed to rely almost wholly on the *All India Reporter* or the *Indian Law Review* to support their arguments. References to what H.M. Seervai or Nani Palkhivala had said in their arguments as well as comments made or questions raised by Justices such as P.N. Bhagwati rang out time and again with no mention of any Pakistani legal luminary to break the flow.

Citations were made of verdicts passed by the superior benches of the Indian judiciary in the weeks and months immediately preceding the hearings in the Pakistani courts. Forty years after the adoption of the Indian Constitution marked our decisive break from the legacy of British-era jurisprudence shared by the whole subcontinent! I would probably have been less taken aback if someone had cited *Itty Pangu Menon v Governor of Madras*, the judgement in an appeal filed by my great-great-grandfather in the 1910s. As I fought off slumber in a sweltering, over-crowded chamber of a Supreme Court that had been barely erected and still required much interior work, a sense of the unreal was sometimes overwhelming.

In terms of their contexts, those two cases did reveal quite sharply that the two countries were very different, although not in the way Pakistanis would have wanted. In the first you had a former army chief being dragged to court in a corruption case. Beg, wearing a smart tweed jacket on most days of his trial, did manage to retain military gravitas. Yet the pathos of a former army chief being hauled over the coals in the courtroom of a country that prides itself on its martial ethos was unmissable. While our reverence for our four stars might not be so openly expressed, the prospect of a general of ours being tried on criminal charges is so excruciating that the government, judiciary and media will put in effort to see that proceedings do not degenerate into a circus. For all the tall talk of their reverence for the military, Pakistani civilians seemed to harbour deep resentment, perhaps even disdain, for their compatriots in uniform.

The second case was even weirder. Prime ministers have been ousted in our country, once within thirteen days. In all cases, however, they went because they had lost majority support in parliament. Sharif was dismissed in the same manner as Benazir three years earlier, because one old curmudgeon took the personal decision that the country needed a new prime minister.

Incidentally, the disdain felt for Ishaq Khan was near universal and much more intense than it was for Gen Beg. Once, Vinod and I got into an exchange with a bunch of Pakistani scribes on the question of which of the two *buddhas*—old men—was the more experienced administrator—our man P.V. Narasimha Rao or Ishaq Khan. The Pakistanis clinched that argument. 'When your man was fighting for freedom, our man was helping the British suppress it.'

There have been a few Indian presidents who were widely despised. Expressions of the sentiment were for the most part unnecessary since our heads of state cannot really do much harm. In contrast, I am willing to wager that outside his family not a single tear was shed for Ishaq Khan when the then army chief General Waheed Kakar sent him packing a few weeks later. Although Kakar ousted Sharif from the prime ministerial chair at the same time, the whole country had been so wearied by the months-long drama and probably so thrilled at seeing Ishaq Khan's back that the army's action met with no protest worth the name.

By the time Sharif filed the petition against his dismissal, much had happened to deflate the triumphalism that his compatriots had been displaying towards India. Our country had not been torn apart by political turmoil or caste/communal conflicts. K.P.S. Gill had won the intra-Jat Sikh war, smashed the Khalistan movement and brought peace to Punjab. Kabul had fallen to the Mujahideen, but not to

Gulbuddin Hekmatyar or another Pakistan proxy. Ahmed Shah Massoud sat on the western side of the Khyber ending the dream of a new empire to be ruled from Islamabad.

These two cases marked the collapse of that particular effort by the Pakistani establishment to bamboozle the people. From 1990 to '93, a myth had been propagated that the military, bureaucracy and loyal politicians were providing united leadership to the nation in a triumphant forward march. By the end of this period, the provincial government in Punjab, headed by Shehbaz Sharif, the Prime Minister's brother, had brought a case against the former army chief. Nawaz Sharif, the one-time golden boy of the establishment, had taken on Ishaq Khan, who had long been regarded as the imperishable wizard of the bureaucracy. And the military had finally packed off these heads of the other two components of the triumvirate. As had happened before and would happen again, the nation had to contemplate the reality that the myth-making had sought to hide.

A glimpse into that reality was provided in the course of the hearings in the dismissal case. Instead of cohesion, what prevailed in the country was fierce competition between disparate interests, each of which would use any means to come out on top. Amidst the jostling for space in the courtroom, I one day found a seat on the side of the Bar's front row. Yahya Bakhtiar, winner of many a legal contest, who apparently preferred to carry his papers in cheap plastic bags, was leading the arguments for Sharif. Until that day, the pronouncements from the Bench had suggested that the Hon'ble Justices were inclined to rule in favour of the deposed Prime Minister.

On that day, however, there was a distinct change in the thrust of Milords' questions. Chief Justice Nassim Hassan Shah, a feisty little man who wore a fez cap and, according to rumour, also used a few cushions to enhance his presence on the Bench, seemed far less perky. As the hearing adjourned for the day, I heard Bakhtiar say to a fellow counsel, 'He seems to have thrown in the towel.'

Bakhtiar was implying that the Permanent Power had pressed the Chief Justice to see the light. A few days later, it appeared that the Ittefaq Group and other conglomerates, with financial clout backing the Muslim League, had applied sufficient counter-pressure to correct the judicial perspective. Or at least, as much was implied by a politician who was once a Sharif acolyte but had since turned against the patron. In conversation with a few press people he went close to committing contempt of court several times before backing off. When I got a moment for a private exchange, I asked the man whether my amplification of his implied comments was accurate. He gave me a pitying look and said, 'You are from India aren't you? Stop asking silly questions like a *gora*.'

For an Indian raised and trained to believe in the probity of our higher judiciary, this imputation of venality shared on both sides of the border was too much to swallow. But I did not rebut the man, and when the Court ruled in favour of Sharif a few days later, felt free to bask in the satisfaction felt by many Pakistanis at a verdict that gave the establishment its comeuppance.

If Ishaq Khan had any sense of constitutional propriety, or even self-respect for that matter, he should have gone away to tend to his rose garden in Bannu. Instead, he seemed to be scouring the bureaucratic handbook to find some obscure precedent which would justify another order dismissing the prime minister. For his part, Sharif refused to quit, inviting the cussed old man to do his worst. Those in the know talk of the comic drama that unfolded over the next few weeks. Apparently, the army chief Gen Waheed Kakar, the then head of ISI and the commander of the Rawalpindi Corps (which has the 111 Brigade—the coup brigade—as one of its component units), embarked on a daily shuffle between Aiwan-e-Sadr (the Presidential palace) and the Prime Minister's House trying to persuade one or the other to relent. Ishaq Khan and Sharif kept playing the reverse of the old courteous Lucknowi nawabs trope—asserting '*Pehle Woh*' instead of '*Pehle Aap*'—until Kakar finally had enough and told them both to pack off on the same day.

Sharif, as the main factor behind Khan's ouster, was actually in a position to face the electorate with a massive achievement in his ledger. As it used to be said in the subcontinent, it is impossible to oust a Kabuliwallah tenant once he settles in your property. Ishaq Khan was from the eastern side of the Durand Line but he brought in as much buttock-weight to cling onto his possession as his legendary Pakhtun brothers from the Afghan capital.

As triumphalism ebbed, there was a twist to the old theme of 'We are not Indians'. It was actually a revival of an old line and shorn of embellishment; how it read was as follows: 'We are bad, but they are no better.' Ayaz Amir, an officer in the air-defence artillery before he turned columnist, never seemed able to shake off the indoctrination he had been subjected to in the Pakistan Military Academy, despite all his other merits.

The Muslim League once rammed a constitutional amendment through the National Assembly in double-quick time. The whole process took twelve minutes from introduction to final vote (I timed it in a feat of perspicacity that I remain proud of). As I staggered out of the Assembly hall, the massively portly correspondent of the *Voice of America* asked me, 'Did an express train rush through right now?'

An equally staggered Amir joined us. He recovered faster than I did and told the American that this was how matters moved in the subcontinent. *Voice of America* was not convinced and asked me for confirmation that in India such would not have happened. It was with some regret at the time that I declined the invitation. From the perspective of 2019, I am glad that I did not express my agreement with the VOA man. The way in which Article 370 was jettisoned was after all no different.

Recent aberrations notwithstanding, India has got more things right than Pakistan has on the whole. That is our belief and any objective study of the record would also bear out this conclusion. What remains is to identify areas in which they have done better. This task was a little easier in the 1990s.

As the last decade of the last century began, the per capita Gross Domestic Product of the two countries was almost on par. A very slight edge that Pakistan had in terms of raw numbers was magnified by the appearance of relative prosperity. Since the *shalwar-kameez* is a full-body outfit that can cover scrawny limbs better than *dhoti-kurta* and since the practice of *zakat* provided the poor with at least one set of fresh clothes a year, signs of abject poverty—which statistics indicated was rampant—were harder to come by west of Wagah.

Roads, especially arterial ones and others likely to be used by bigwigs and outsiders, were usually of slicker construction than ours with the Grand Trunk and the Pindi–Murree roads quite outstanding. For travel between the cities there were medium-sized vans called 'flying coaches', which in the days before the arrival of Volvo buses, were quite a revelation. Our Maruti revolution had started barely years before and we trailed way behind when it came to matters of style on the road. (A small consolation was that our autorickshaws were better than the execrable knee-crunchers plying about in Lahore and elsewhere.)

Their textiles were better in both material and stitching. For proof of the first, I need only remember the length of time for which I used some of the T-shirts I bought during my stint. As for the latter, I could go by the reception Nandini got whenever she put on one of her made-in-Pakistan outfits while on holiday back home. Our tailors took another decade to catch up. In those days we had to rely on our movie stars to stay on par with them in the glamour stakes. Indians born after the economic liberalization might not believe and those born before might have forgotten that there was a time when we had resigned ourselves to playing catch-up to the Asian Tigers.

This is only a random flip through not a full catalogue of relative merits but it cannot be let go without a mention of Janab Anwar Rathore. For some reason that still bewilders me, I did not like ripe mangoes until my mid-thirties. After that I became an *aam*-fanatic but by then I had suffered grievous losses. I did not get my fill of the basketloads produced in my father-in-law's farm before he sold the land and I do not remember the taste of Pakistan's best variety. They swore by it.

'You can keep your nukes,' Haqqani boasted on a day long before the 1998 tests. 'You will never touch us so long as we have our Anwar Rathores.'

Apart from the easier availability of dry fruit, Pakistan would appear to have lost almost all other advantages between then and now. India's GDP growth graph began veering away from the mid-1990s and there is near forty-five-degree difference between the two lines on a grid sheet. From what one can decipher from TV images, the visual contrast seems just as sharp. If the weaponry, especially F-16 combat aircraft, granted to them by their Afghan war allies, gave reason for panache at that time, the arrival of the MIG-29s, Su-30s and now the first batch of Rafales seems to signify an erasure of that reason for swagger.

Our fighting men never had much use for Pakistani pretensions anyway. Once, I accompanied our Air and Navy attachés to a rehearsal of the Pakistan Day parade. First to come on were the SSG men—the Special Service Group, or the special forces of the Pakistan Army—in their camouflage uniforms, double-time march and chants of 'Ali, Ali' on every fourth step. 'Louts,' was the comment from our uniformed stalwarts.

To close the parade, the Pakistan Air Force put on a fly past. Its finale was a 'vertical charlie' by a lone F-16. The fighter jet roared up to a point about three hundred feet above the reviewing stand, tilted its nose upwards and shot off in an incredibly fast corkscrew to disappear into the cloud haze. I turned my awestruck gaze to our two fighter pilots—the Navyman was a carrier flyer—only to find them grinning at me.

'Impressed?' Group Captain (later Air Marshal) Satish Jain asked me. When I said I was, he and Anil Bakshi educated me. They, the Indians, that is, had been trained to make a slow approach to the vertical shoot-off point of the manoeuvre and to accelerate into the climb. 'What this guy did was something like throwing a stone from a slingshot. The momentum was already there.'

Even in those days, there would sometimes be a lightning flash illumination of a realism underlying the bombast. After Nawaz Sharif won the court case and was restored to power at the centre, he needed to oust the Ishaq Khan-installed governor in Punjab. The order appointing this governor was revoked but the man refused to vacate the governor's mansion. Sharif pressed the chief minister to do whatever was needed. There was only so much that the man could do and was driven to exasperation by the demands of the national leadership.

When the suggestion finally came that he use the police to storm official buildings, the man apparently threw up his hands exclaiming. 'Who does he think I am? Shivaji?'

Yes! The reference was to the Chhatrapati Maharaj and it was an admission that the Hindu could perform superior feats of heroism.

~

None of this provides any justification for our tendency to underestimate Pakistan. If nothing else we need to remember that *jugaad* is a South Asian talent not an exclusively Indian one. Or honestly admit that reverse swing was a Pakistani invention. A recent comment by one of our cricketers that Pakistani pacemen would not allow anyone to touch the shiny side of the ball with wet palms reveals the extent to which they had perfected the art.

Arrival at the art of reverse swing was not a chance development. There is a sociology to it. I have played street football so I know that this particular school teaches you skills not taught in formal coaching systems. You learn how to drop your shoulder and then jerk up in a smashing movement at the perfect moment to jostle your opponent of the ball; to use knees, elbows and tripping feet without getting caught by the cheating-alert other side; when to trade a foul and penalty to deny a rival a clear shot and so on. These skills are all taught by on-field mentors and Pakistani society appears to have instinctively crafted this brotherly habit into systems.

My friend and neighbour Naqvi Saab had a fair-sized brood of sons from two wives (consecutive not concurrent). The second boy from the second marriage was a tearaway quick. He was not tall or particularly well-built at that time but he could still fire a frightening bouncer off the asphalt of our street. I have no idea whether he made his way to any team of significance. In either case, no one could blame his elder half-brothers who worked on his grip, action, run-up and so on constantly and got friends over ever so often to do the same.

It was not only a matter of sibling bonding. In fact, brotherly feelings seemed just a part of the reason for so much help being given to the youngster. It was more like a talent had been spotted and everyone who could wanted to make a contribution. We would do well to remember that this collective drive to nourish and preserve rare resources or talents can be brought to bear in other fields, not just cricket.

As mentioned earlier, Pakistan got its nukes without going through the elaborate and painstaking methods we did. Steel of a particular quality was obtained from some source; the rods were turned into centrifuge arrays according to a design stolen from somewhere else; enriched uranium spat out by the array was moulded into a bomb configuration in accord with a model begged and borrowed from yet another source. As with the warheads, so with the fifty-year-old Mirage Rose-1 aircrafts that are still being kept aloft by the master craftsmen in the Kamra Aeronautical Complex.

There is a directness of approach combined with an all-or-nothing effort to get what they want. In the early days of my stay in Pakistan, there was some amazement among our High Commission staff at the discovery that the Pakistan navy had managed to retrofit the Harpoon cruise missile so that these anti-ship rockets could be launched from the torpedo tubes of submarines. Science and engineering education in the country was too poor to have allowed them to pull off the feat, was the general opinion. I too started parroting the amazed tones until I was brought up short by our own sailor Arjun Sreedharan.

'Why are you so surprised?' Arjun asked me. 'After all, they have the same brains as we do.'

Living With the Enemy

One morning in May 1998, I backed my car out of the garage of our Bahrain residence without checking to see that all doors were shut and was soundly punished for the idiocy. The right rear door swung open just in time for its edge to catch a pillar and get nicely mangled. For reasons that have long been erased from memory, I was in desperate need of wheels for the next few days and rental agencies were not able to help. Every friend I spoke to in the auto business, pointed me in the same direction. If I wanted the car back by the evening, I would have to call the Pakistani garage.

Two men came with a tow truck and took the car away, telling me to collect it that evening. I got down to the daily routine of monitoring events, reading up, making phone calls and so on. By evening came the news that Pakistan had conducted nuclear tests in Chagai, Balochistan. The frisson of excitement at this development set off a chain of thought that ended with an image of Anwar Mansoori, Pakistan correspondent of Deustche Presse Agentur.

Mansoori was one of those wonderful souls whom no one could ever consider an enemy. Usually he would greet us Indian correspondents when we dropped by with a calm smile that gave no indication of the enormous cordiality that he never failed to offer. One day he looked unusually pensive. When asked why he said that he had been worrying about the implications that the rivalry between India and Pakistan would have for his children. Would they face the threat of a nuclear war? Five or six years after that day, Mansoori's nightmare had cast off the mooring line that kept it tethered to the gravity field of the theoretical.

My car was more than ready when I got to the garage. Not only had the dents been smoothened and the door painted but the whole machine had been scrubbed down as well. The ten or dozen tough-looking workmen had finished for the day and were sipping tea sitting on benches a few feet away from the office cabin. They all shot curious looks my way but not the snide or anti-India remarks I had half expected. All of them were in Awami, bar the office manager who led me inside to settle the bill. When I stepped out after making the payment, the devil in me rose to the surface.

'*Aap logon ne bhi phod diya?*' (You people exploded it too?) I asked him within hearing of his compatriots.

'*Kya karein? Aap logon ke peeche peeche.*' (What else to do? We had to follow you people.) We exchanged rueful chuckles and parted.

This episode can be cited as a sample of the ways in which Indians and Pakistanis can get along in places outside the subcontinent even in times of high tension. Actually, I did not have much to do with people from other parts of South Asia after my Pakistan stint. A couple of seminars with representatives from several countries; a visit to Chennai by the duo who ran *Friday Times*; two or three travel-time friendships struck up while waiting for flights; and interactions with two Sri Lankan maids and a Bangladeshi gardener are about all that come to mind. As West Asia correspondent of an Indian newspaper, based in Bahrain to boot, I was not integral to any of the journalistic fraternities that covered that part of the world. Nor was I part of any professional circle—doctors, accountants, bankers, executives—more common in the Gulf. Indian friends of mine did interact with Pakistanis and they did not give the impression that nationality intruded into the relationships to any great extent.

That in any case is not the point. What people in India want to know when I tell them that I once lived in Pakistan is something very specific. They want to find out what life is like for an Indian in that country. One answer straight-up is that it is profoundly different because of one essential, inescapable element, no matter all the commonalties. What is basic to an Indian's existence in Pakistan—the inescapable element—is that he/she is not a citizen of that country. How that makes for a massive difference from normal existence will be dealt with later. For the moment it is sufficient to say that, for all the cultural affinities, he or she is not a citizen and hence does not have many of the rights conferred by that status. An Indian in Pakistan soon discovers that the tectonic plates under his feet are diabolical. So long as they remain stable, life can be pleasant. When they convulse, and they can do so very suddenly, life can be downright ugly.

In taking up the good times to start with, it is best that I go back to my landlord, Pir Nazakat Shah. Not only was he one of my first acquaintances, later one of my first friends in that country, he was also the first to demonstrate that the hugeness of the Punjabi heart is not constricted by the border.

House hunting was a daunting prospect at first because I was suddenly faced with a life-transforming upgrade from the second-floor *barsati* in Safdarjung Enclave which was all I could afford as a correspondent with the Delhi bureau. It was a nice apartment for a newly-married couple with a balcony fronting a hall divided into two by a hardboard partition, a small functional kitchen and a large back terrace with a strategically located *ghusalkhana*.

Those kinds of digs would hardly do in the new situation where I had become the face of a revered paper. Islamabad, perhaps more so than most other capitals, was an extremely status-conscious city, mainly because it was crammed to the pine tips with bureaucrats, the most social-grade-conscious genus of the human species.

Prestige had to be maintained and G. Kasturi, *The Hindu*'s Editor, let me know that the purse-strings were loose. That was all very well, except for the fact that I had never set eyes on the amounts involved. Pir Saab, if I remember right, wanted a full year's rent of more than two lakhs in advance and accepted Rs 10,000 or so as a token payment. Then the trouble started.

For some convoluted reason, the cheque was sent to Karachi for clearance and disappeared into a monetary dark-hole. Extremely helpful staff in the Islamabad and Rawalpindi branches of ANZ Grindlays helped me track it down but the pinstripe at the other end refused to budge. By then, I had both overshot Pir Saab's deadline and was desperately low on funds for personal needs in a place where I knew only a few and none well enough to borrow from.

On a day when I had been assured that the cash would show up in my account, the Pir came early to the guesthouse where I was staying. We went to ANZ in Islamabad. No luck. ANZ Pindi, ditto. By then, I was so down in spirits that I was sure the Pir was suspicious of me and so took what I thought was the best way out. You can cancel the lease, I told him, and if possible return some of the money I had advanced so that I could hang on or go back.

'*Aapke pas paise nahi hain?*' he asked me very concerned. (You do not have money?) I replied that I had a little and so on, shame making a hash of my attempt to show that I had matters in hand. He caught on that I was dithering and pulled over to the side of the road. Without another word, he unclasped the top button of his *kameez*, dug out a money bag and thrust ten thousand rupees into my hand, refusing to countenance any protest. When I had run through that sum, he told me, I could ask him for more.

A man he had never known before. Someone who could disappear into the Indian High Commission and from there scoot out of Pakistan for ever. Perhaps the amount was not large given his wealth. That was hardly the point. Needless to say it came as a huge relief when the bank called a day or two later to announce that the funds had arrived.

Pir Saab usually took care of any minor repairs that needed to be done and was absolutely straight about what I had to pay for. Our friendship grew and then got truly nourished. He was a *Sajjada Nashin* (descendant of the founder-saint and hence chief trustee) of Bade Imam, one of the most important *dargahs* of the Potohar. Not very familiar with the culture of Sufism as I was then and full of ideas about Shariah-imposed restrictions, I had taken some pains to keep him from knowing that I had liquor stored in the house. Pir Saab was not fooled; perhaps it was one of the reasons he wanted me as a tenant. Before that year's Urs began, he asked me whether I could arrange for some stocks. When I went for the ceremony, I understood where he was coming from.

They came from all over the Potohar and Hazara. Hordes of them in great groups, carrying massive *chadors* and smashed out of their heads. Stoned on *hashish* and *bhang* certainly, probably floating on home-brewed moonshine as well. A case of the best vodka from Murree Distillery and the few bottles of Scotch I had arranged for the Pir would probably not have lasted for more than that evening. Guilt at poor service remained with me for the rest of my stint and I did my best to make sure to keep some stock aside for the Pir every month.

Alcohol could smoothen social relationships in a very handy way at that time. With generosity and understanding, the authorities had allowed foreign correspondents to access duty-free shops and bonded warehouses and the High Commission was always the court of last resort. Quotas were fairly liberal and this did lead to misuse. Some of the smaller diplomatic missions were notorious for doing brisk business in the stuff though perhaps none reached the scale of a certain Southeast Asian country's embassy in Saudi Arabia. This mission in Riyadh, so goes the folklore, apparently got a call from Saudi customs by which it was informed that the container of furniture that it was trying to bring in 'was leaking'.

Abuse apparently did reach worrisome levels at least on one occasion during my stay in Pakistan. This led the then chief of protocol, a Christian retired Colonel, to trim the quota marginally. Irritated diplomats promptly labelled the measure the 'Tesslor Amendment' in honour of the Colonel. It was also a nod at the US Congressman Larry Pressler who had inserted a clause into the military aid law that such assistance would be contingent on a presidential certification that Pakistan was not pursuing a nuclear weapons programme.

Non-Muslims, including Pakistanis, were also allowed to buy six or eight bottle lots every month from the outlets of local distillers, mainly Murree Brewery. To avail of the quotas the buyer had to go through the small inconvenience of filling a form to obtain a permit. Appropriate columns could be filled in English, though everyone was conscious of the import of the first two lines in Urdu. They read: '*Sharaabi ka tarruf*' and '*Sharaabi ke walid ka tarruf*'. As someone said, it would have been nice if liquor could have been bought without associating your father with it.

Muslim Pakistanis had their own ways of getting the stuff. Bootleggers would make the rounds each evening, taking orders and payment in advance for assured home delivery.

Vodka and rum were my preferences but higher-grade liquor was available. Veteran journalist, and whisky connoisseur, T.V.R. Shenoy was offered something special when he visited the offices of Murree Brewery. Shenoy Saab took a sip, rolled it around his palate and pronounced to the gratification of his hosts that it tasted like a Lowland malt. That was precisely what experts from Scotland had told the Murree men.

Pir Saab had told mc at the time of the Urs that there was no point looking for him at the *dargah* and that I should instead visit his house later on. It was one of the most pleasant evenings I ever had, even though spent in total sobriety. Perhaps because the Pir's farmhouse was one of the most serene settings I have ever been in.

His house was not modest in size though simple in construction, very homely and welcoming like Punjabi farmsteads usually are. Creepers climbed the pillars to the slanting rood of the porch, flower-pots of varying sizes sprouted haphazardly and water had been sprinkled on the packed earth. About half-a-dozen men from the village were in attendance and we sat around on cane chairs sipping tea and shooting the early winter breeze.

As I slipped into a convivial mood, insights into life in that farmstead formed unbidden. For one, though the women of the house did not come out there was a voice—strong, loud, unmistakably matronly and assertive enough to repeatedly draw the Pir's attention—which made clear that the village head was far from an unchallenged patriarch. The second surprise was even more soothing. Instead of rushing for their prayer rugs when the *azaan* was called, the men made small gestures—catching their earlobes and so on—and muttered a *sura* or so before returning to the conversation. They probably did a proper *wuzu* and went through the protocols of the *namaaz* before dinner on returning to their own houses. But for the moment, their duties as hosts came foremost.

The gathering broke up gradually as twilight set in, men moving out after hand-to-chest farewells. It was the essence of rural South Asia, a feeling of wholesomeness that I had felt and learnt to cherish at my grandmother's house in Ponnani. Her brothers and cousins would gather in her verandah after visiting the temple, chat for a while and then depart for their own residences. Farm-workers arriving at intervals, weary voices, rattling of rails in the cattle shed, the crash and clatter of implements being dumped punctuating the end of the rural day. A pattern of rural life, varying in detail and similar in essence, stretching from the northern end of the subcontinent to the southern.

~

Friendship with the Pir involved the traverse of several social barriers and could not probably have been sustained in another context. It was impossible to imagine him staying with a real sense of comfort for more than a couple of days, if that, in any flat I had in Delhi. Confinement to a few rooms in a building with other families living close by would have been very uncomfortable for this country-bred man. We, as a middle-class Indian working couple, would probably also have felt that we were walking on eggshells with a conservative Pakistani sharing our space. Reciprocation from our side, in the same manner as the hospitality the Pir extended, would have been at one remove at best. Such an arrangement could not have made for a lasting, deepening bond.

For reasons that will become clear in the next chapter, life-long relationships were forged with families of the Indian High Commission officials. These were of the nature of bonds between people who have faced very tough experiences together. We Indian journalists formed a group of our own within that slightly larger community. When I first arrived in Islamabad, the Indian contingent consisted of Mohan Narayan (Press Trust of India), V.K. Dethe (*Times of India*) and Suresh Chopra (AIR/Doordarshan). A year and a half later Mohan had been replaced by Sujit Chatterjee, Dethe by Sunil Narula, and Vinod Sharma (*Hindustan Times*) had arrived as a pioneer for his paper. As Sri Lankans, the Ranawanas did not share all those trials but Arjuna and Shyama were roughly of the same age, we had journalism backgrounds in common and their three little youngsters were a joy to us who were childless at the time.

These three sets of relationships were each based on something tangible from which further bonds developed. A host–tenant nexus in the case of the Pir, age and professional parity with the Ranawanas and a search for security through solidarity with the Indians. No pragmatic basis of this sort underlay the very special relations we had with a group Nandini and I referred to as our Three Old Men. A.B.S. Jaffri, A.H. Rizvi and Naqvi Saab were a threesome to delight the heart. (I am ashamed to admit that I cannot now recollect Naqvi Saab's initials and have no way of finding out either.) Collectively, they were avuncular mentors who guided us in the ways of Pakistan with nudges and winks; raconteurs of lore that clarified quirks of the society we found ourselves in; possessors of impish wit that deflated pretensions of the powerful on both sides of the border; and providers of a haven from the tensions of living in hostile territory. Theirs was a friendship freely given for no discernible reason and with great potential for damage to themselves.

Jaffri Saab was at that time the Editor of *The Muslim*. He had come to the post after a long stint as Editor of *Kuwait Times* and an even longer innings as a political reporter with connections to the highest echelons of his country. When I say connections, I do not say so lightly. He had been Pakistan's first ever foreign correspondent when he was posted in Delhi and had moved on to become Resident Editor of *Pakistan Times* in Rawalpindi. Perhaps the post was less important than the fact that he had been a drinking buddy, or perhaps junior companion, to Zulfiqar Ali Bhutto and Yahya Khan. He had also been a cricket commentator until a medical problem frayed his vocal chords. The hoarse whisper that rasped out from the 'collar' he wore on his throat actually enhanced his charm.

Mrs Jaffri had an equally colourful background. She was Bengali by ethnicity and had been an Awami League Member of the National Assembly elected from a constituency in East Pakistan. Her family was heavily connected to powerful clans there, including the Suhrawardis and others of that pedigree. They lived with their daughter in a modest but lovely bungalow in one of the western sectors of Islamabad and on most Fridays, before noon, I would get the summons.

'What are you doing at home? Today is Jumma. Come for prayers.' There he would be waiting for us with a mischievous smile on his face, impeccably groomed and fastidiously dressed. Messrs Rizvi and Naqvi would have either already arrived by then or would show up soon after and proceedings would get underway. I cannot recollect how we worked it out but the operations always went along without hitches. Either I got the vodka or he did and if one brought the booze, the other provided the *nihari.* Mrs Jaffri would add on some other eats and if Mrs Naqvi, a great cook, got into the act, succulent Awadhi *kababs* would be added to the repertoire.

Conversation flowed fast and smooth and ranged over all manner of subjects. If there was a cricket match involving Pakistan or India on at the time, the telecast would play out without really intruding. It was one place where you could watch an India–Pakistan match in a civilized manner with respect for good performances on either side and laughter at foibles no matter who committed them. A couple of examples of their sense of humour should provide an inkling of the reason for arriving at such comfort levels.

Four of us, on a boys' evening out, are at the house of a retired bureaucrat when the phone rings in the hallway and neither host nor hostess are to be seen. Naqvi goes out, answers the call and returns to the drawing room with the announcement, '*Begum ka bulawa hai.*' (You have been summoned by the lady.)

The message was meant for Jaffri but Naqvi's eyes are fixed on Rizvi's face when he makes the announcement.

'*Yeh toh hairaani ki baat hai,*' says Rizvi, straight-faced, with a hand on his chest. (That is shocking indeed.) Chuckles all round. Rizvi's wife had passed away a few years earlier.

On another occasion, a Japanese journalist who is interviewing Jaffri asks him for his assessment of the Kashmir problem.

'There is no problem,' says Jaffri.

'How can you say that? The two armies can clash at any time,' says the daughter of Nippon.

'When a situation remains unchanged for forty-five years, it is not a problem,' says Jaffri. 'It is a part of life.'

The instances on which the Three Old Men helped me settle my mind and spirit are too numerous to recount. In any case, it was the overall welcome they extended that meant more than any specific assistance. Professionally, it helped that they represented three different shades of view within a general matrix of liberalism. Naqvi was a bureaucrat with the Tourism Department and not in the same league in terms of political analysis as the other two. He was, however, a staunch PPP man and also had connections with the MQM. That enabled me to keep in some sort of touch with the mid-level attitudes in both parties.

Rizvi, then head of Pakistan Press International (the *other* news agency) was an epitome of distilled journalistic world-weariness who had soured on all parties as well as the 'Guardians'. His instincts were exceptionally acute since he seemed to sniff out Nawaz Sharif's rebellious itch long before most had any notion of it. Enthusiasms were quite alien to his nature so whenever he did succumb it only needed Jaffri to say with a long-suffering tone, 'Afzar Hussain Rizvi,' for this gentleman to resume his cynical persona.

Jaffri was the philosopher who had seen and heard it all. With his finely honed skill in the art of the gentle put down, which he deployed against his country's and his newspaper's management, this wise old man could help younger professionals fixate on what was important.

They had a suave way of dealing with and helping me deal with phases of menace, which I shall describe in the next chapter. There were periods in time when hostility between the two countries reached such a fever pitch that normal relations between people became impossible. But theirs would be an attitude comprised of regret, realism and the recognition that our friendship would eventually prevail. 'This will pass. Let's wait it out,' was how Jaffri put it the first time and we learnt to slip into that mode.

~

A western journalist, Christina Lamb I think it was, has written about the freemasonry of the journalistic community. This is particularly potent in the subcontinent. As a metro-based journalist who would frequently parachute into the bailiwick of State-, district- and taluk-level correspondents, I had learnt to respect the bonds of the *biradari* for the lifeline they were. There were so many occasions on which a reporter in Bastar or Amritsar re-adjusted his schedule so that he could show the city-slicker the ropes that only a fool or a knave could have failed to develop genuine respect for these relatively unheralded soldiers of the profession.

On the night of 30–31 October 1984, I caught a night bus from Jagdalpur in Bastar to Raipur, the nearest railhead. My idea was to catch the afternoon Chhattisgarh Express so as to arrive in Bhopal by the morning of 1 November, spend a couple of days in that city and then move on to Delhi. With time on my hands, I called friends in *Dainik Bhaskar*. Instead of the usual friendly banter they told me to come over immediately. When I got there, they handed me the 'takes' fresh off the agency wires that reported the shooting of Mrs Indira Gandhi by her bodyguards. The news would probably have come to my attention within an hour or so anyway but I could also have well missed it for longer in the process of checking out of the hotel and boarding the train. The ways of the freemasonry dictated that the lady reporter on duty at the *Bhaskar* bureau alert me as soon as I got in touch.

The bonds stretched across the border. On the night when the army chief Gen Waheed Kakar packed off both Ishaq Khan and Nawaz Sharif a restlessness that had no discernible cause drove me to the Islamabad office of *Dawn* well after I had finished my supper. '*Idhar kya kar rahe ho? Aiwan-e-Sadr jao. Khabar toh wahin ban rahi hai,*' said the lone correspondent co-ordinating coverage from the office. (What are you doing here? Go to the Aiwan-e-Sadr—the Presidential house. That's where you'll get the latest.) We Indian correspondents had not been informed that Gen Kakar had come to a momentous decision and got the interim President Wassim Sajjad (otherwise the Chairman of the Senate—the upper house of Pakistan's parliament) to summon the national media to announce it. Alerted, it was my turn to inform Vinod, Sunil and Sujit who were all at the Central Telegraph Office. No one stopped us from entering the Presidential Palace and we hence got a ringside view of the goings on.

To a degree, the *biradari*'s benefits were accorded only

to genuine reporters and extended by those of the same ilk. It is something that even people who have entered the profession laterally and not worked their way from the ground up do not really catch on to. Once at a seminar in Delhi, two bigshots from the Pakistani and Lankan media openly asked whether an Indian correspondent in Pakistan (or vice versa) could really do very much. As an amateur in the talking-head game, I could only stutter the answer that I had not felt a professional stranger because of the help I had got from my Pakistani colleagues. Sardonic smiles were all I got for my pains on that occasion.

How can you explain to others the value of a tip-off? Or the invitation to have a quick look at notes taken during a briefing to which you were not invited. Or the hint that what you had been told by an official in ostensibly utter sincerity had already been contradicted by developments elsewhere. An example in reverse might give some idea of what I am talking about.

In Casablanca, for an Organization of the Islamic Conference meet, a Pakistani friend drew me aside and asked, '*Kya tum yeh pura cover karne ja rahe ho?*' (Do you intend to cover this in detail?)

I said I did since I had travelled on company money. Well, said my friend, he had come on a government junket and he was damned if he was going to miss the chance to see Fez, Marrakesh and Tangier. A look at the street life in those cities would not only be far more enjoyable, it would also do him a lot more professional good than taking notes at a boring conference. There was hardly a chance that he would visit those places on his own. So could I give him my copy in the evening? Sure, I would, but the story would have an Indian angle.

'Koi baat nahi, yaar. Main usko Pakistani twist de doonga.' (No problem. I will give it a Pakistani twist.) The scheme worked.

A lot of the work that an Indian journalist—any foreign correspondent for that matter—can do in Pakistan is perforce second-hand. Even international news agencies do not have the spread to cover every district in the country, nor enough personnel in the national headquarters to keep tabs on all major news sources. Foreigners have to rely on local news organizations to keep updated with events and developments. To illustrate, we can advert to the relatively recent example of the Indian Air Force's raid on Balakot.

We do not know for sure whether it was a panic call from a local resident in Balakot or the official communiqué from the government of India that set off this particular news cycle. Whatever the spark-off might have been, the office of a news agency (say, Reuters) in Islamabad would have tried to first get an idea of what had actually happened and gone on to obtain confirmation and further details. It is a safe bet that Reuters's network of stringers did not extend beyond Abbottabad, the district headquarters of Hazara, if even that. Like all other media outfits, including the bulk of the national organizations, resort would have been made to the wider network of the Associated Press of Pakistan. (Before the computer age, the teleprinter machine that ran news agency feeds held a sacred space in major news offices. Not all news offices, since the hire of the agency services made it a fairly expensive proposition.)

Reuters, Islamabad would have also called their people in

Peshawar, who would have called Abbottabad who in turn could have reached out to a local contact in the vicinity of Balakot. If this last contact was a government functionary or someone used to dealing with officialdom, confirmation and further details might have been forthcoming. If not, the contact-of-a-contact chain would have needed to be extended further. Another or other chains would have been simultaneously activated with a view to obtaining further corroboration.

But journalistic networks can almost never beat the official channels in speed and mass of detail. In military matters, even a rough sketch of events cannot be drawn without knowledge of the terrain, techniques and tactics. News organizations also come into possession of granular details of major non-military events such as natural disasters much more gradually than the official machinery. Usually, on macro-events of this sort, the narrative that first takes shape is the official and that cannot be easily shaken.

Government schemes and policies are the red rags to the journalistic bull in democracies. There were a few Pakistanis who tried to go behind and beyond the pronouncements and claims put out by the government on economic matters. (Farhan Bokhari is the one name that comes to mind. I can't quite recall which paper he worked for then, though it was probably *The News*.) These stories could be mined for a lot of useful data but the rest of the media hardly ever got on to the task of running the leads down. Probably, in the same mode as us outsiders, local journalists were overwhelmed by the cascades of political developments.

Politics is the field where journalists really come into

their own. National or regional, it is a subject that really gets the journalistic juices flowing, a field in which you have to develop and deploy a range of professional skills. Among them, the abilities to penetrate diverse social clusters; tackle all manner of personalities; cultivate contacts while striking the right balance between intimacy and distance; remember masses of detail; sniff out when you are being taken for a ride; stay in step with the wiliest of characters; be sensitive to changes in relationships between the people you study, knowing full well that alliances are always in flux; and, above all, know where power is pooling at any given time.

It also helps that prime political reporters are accorded much prestige. The wide range of skills and qualities the exercise of which political reporting requires means that anyone who excels can claim star status within the profession. The question of where power is located is one that readers want, and need, to know. So, a journalist who can deliver has reason to be satisfied that his or her primary duty is being fulfilled.

Party statements and communiqués mean very little when they are presented bereft of context. Very often such pronouncements can be misleading or have little connection with the truth. This was in some ways fortuitous for an Indian correspondent in Pakistan because a feel for subcontinental politics provides an advantage that no other foreigner could hope to match.

It must have taken me more than six months to mentally map the political landscape of Pakistan. With two major centrist parties, at least three representing secular but ethno-nationalist strains, an equal number of religious outfits and factions in each and every one of them, time was needed to match names, faces and labels until they were amenable to instant recollection. These details were essential because they together formed the grid that made everything else understandable.

While politics in that country was very much about the machinations of the establishment, the workings of the hidden force could only be followed through the overt actions of those it manipulated. Through the connecting of the dots between what was known about the antecedents and character of a particular politician or party; its closeness or otherwise to the hidden power; the discernible objectives of players involved; and the logic of the situation it would be possible to trace the agenda that was unfolding.

Journalism of this nature apparently reached its apogee among foreigners, based in Hong Kong and later Beijing, who were trying to follow developments in the People's Republic of China. Appropriately enough, this methodology is called 'reading the tea leaves'. Esoteric as it sounds, skill in this art form does produce real results.

For me, a typical working day would begin with a thorough reading of five English papers, go on to checks with the knowledgeable whether something special had appeared in the Urdu press and periodic monitorings of radio and TV. Reports in one paper would have to be compared with corresponding items in the others to ascertain the authentic. Biases of each news outlet as well as its correspondents had become gradually apparent and these would have to be navigated. Theories thus formed would need to be vetted by reliable Pakistani colleagues and because of the phone taps such exchanges would have to be conducted person to person.

Sometimes, the apparently straight-forward served as a smokescreen. On one occasion, perhaps in early 1993, a high-ranking Russian official came on a visit. Since this was not long after the collapse of the Soviet Union, it was significant and the Pakistani Foreign Ministry made much of this new dawn in bilateral relations, putting out a release broadly setting out the areas of agreement. There was a shock waiting for me when I asked the High Commission for its comments.

Apparently, the language of the release had many points in common with the Treaty of Peace, Friendship and Cooperation that Indira Gandhi and Leonid Brezhnev had negotiated in 1971, which assured India of Soviet support for our Bangladesh policy. That Russian's visit actually had far more potentially dangerous consequences for India than I had initially perceived. A faithful ally seemed to be offering an equal friendship to our bitter adversary. That danger passed both because the Russian instigator of the plan fell out of favour with Boris Yeltsin and because Pakistan was soon embroiled in squabbles between the President and the Prime Minister. For a brief moment I could still draw gratification from my role in informing compatriots about something they really needed to know.

Domestic Pakistani politics could also create what can be called 'crises of interpretation'. A case in point was the outbreak of the squabble that led through a few twists and turns to the ouster of Ishaq Khan and Sharif. That matters had deteriorated to such an extent between the President and the Prime Minister was so difficult to believe—given that Khan had been the one to raise Sharif to prominence—that I was not sure if I could go ahead and report that the decisive point had been reached when Sharif made a special appearance on TV to announce, '*Mai kisi ka dictation nahi loonga.*' (I will not be dictated to.) I took my case to Rizvi Saab who confirmed my conclusion by flatly stating, 'What else can it mean?'

Before sending my dispatch I had to go to the High Commission for some matter and was told that His Excellency wanted to see me. Mr Lambah was facing the same dilemma as I had been. He had concluded that the clash had reached the breaking point but all his officers were advising caution. Lambah Saab wanted to know what I thought but since there were others in the office and I did not want my new-found certainty to be disturbed by a debate, told him that I would phone him as soon as I got home. When I called to say, 'Sir, he is going,' Mr Satinder Lambah replied in a tone of great relief, 'Thank you, Keshav. I wanted at least one person to back me up.'

Interpretative reports that annoyed those in power could be hazardous. Even physically so as proved by the ordeals undergone by at least three leading Pakistani journalists during my stint. Foreign journalists did not have diplomatic immunity but the status could offer a measure of protection, up to a point. As a last resort they could cancel out visas and that is not as innocuous as it sounds. You would have a tough time explaining to your superiors the failure of instinct or lack of judgement that resulted in a loss of significant investment. Instinct and judgement are intrinsic to the practice of the profession so question marks about either are highly damaging to your reputation.

Given the visa restrictions, there was really not much scope for investigative journalism, let alone the boondocks and 'blood and guts' varieties. To investigate any matter, the journalist has to invest huge amounts of time cultivating sources. With Indian journalists carrying the enemy tag around with them, no authoritative source would risk the passing on of information. Stories on the economy or society would have to be done by gleaning through the public record.

A set of articles that I did on feudalism and the associated problem of dacoity comes to mind. This is a subject that Indian readers always have time for so inspiration was derived when the tele-series *Chand Grehan* touched upon it. There had been a detailed article in one of the magazines, *Herald* or *Newsline,* as well as a series in *Frontier Post* (if I remember right). These archives provided the bulk of the raw material. Supplemented by conversations with Pakistani journalists and social workers familiar with the subjects, I could at least make an attempt at off-beat journalism without leaving the track.

Election time in 1990 and 1993 provided some scope for trips into the boondocks. These forays could not be too extensive in either time or space but they could at least provide a taste of the ground reporting that I had become so accustomed to before my foreign assignment.

Another form of journalism that combines the adrenaline surges of physical danger and heightened sense awareness is the coverage of riots and police actions. Tear gas grenades and pelted stones do not discriminate between participants and onlookers, especially those in the thick of action. On these kind of jobs you really need three-dimensional vision since the thing that can hurt you could come from any direction. There were a couple of marches to the parliament led by Benazir that ended in lathi charges and a few images remain in the mind.

On both occasions, Benazir took inordinate amounts of time to emerge from her residence to lead the faithful. She was of course covered from top to toe and therefore I could not be certain but a sudden appearance in weight gain seemed to suggest that there were layers of padding hidden inside her clothes. On both occasions she was taken into custody and whistled away in police jeeps. The second image that remains is that of Farooq Leghari, who took over lead of the processions (he was to become President of Pakistan years later), backed up against a van summoning all the authority as feudal lord to warn policemen to stay away from him. One of those processions actually reached the parliament and there was a sudden spectacle of politicians, bureaucrats and journalists who had gathered to watch the fun scrambling for cover as the police began tossing gas grenades.

Developments that unfold at a distance from wherever you are located can be covered second hand. Stationed in Islamabad, you have to depend on sources in Lahore or Karachi to find out the details of events that occur in those cities and cross-checking does not go far most of the time. However, as your understanding builds, you feel that you are getting close to the truth more often than not. In order to build that understanding you need to be constantly engaged. Your mind has to continuously throw up questions that you apply to the facts. To give an example, I can refer to a theory about Pakistan army officers that has probably done the rounds a few times over the years.

The theory is that many of them are the sons of Junior Commissioned Officers who were educated in the army school system (akin to our Sainik Schools). Because of this humbler middle-class background, the theory goes on, they were more conservative and hence more prone to the influence of fundamentalist ideologies. If true, this was a perspective changing theory since it demolished long-standing notions about feudal elites, the continuing impact of Sandhurst or Chetwode Hall and so on.

This is not the kind of conceptualization that an Indian journalist can check on first hand because the barrier of distrust is at its thickest in this area. So you cast your mind over the officers that you have seen close by at airports, public functions and so on. You re-collect images of their *dupatta*-free, stylish-in-deportment wives; remember the Lawrence or Aitchison College accents in which some of them spoke; and recall the sight of them in the Rawalpindi Club or on the Golf Course in T-shirted civvies. When you do so, you find that the 'JCO-sons' hypothesis does not really fit.

Then you test your own presumptions, drawing from your exposure to Indian military men. Yes, you recall, there were people whose mofussil or otherwise modest backgrounds you could discern. But those men too had imbibed much of the culture that had been dominant in their institution for so long. Military personnel are continuously being trained in different skills at different institutions, sometimes abroad. Exposure to different sub-cultures at the least, if not whole milieus, is constant. These are professional people who will try to tick off as many boxes as they can while advancing in their careers. Thereby you come to your own theory that irrespective of family background, Pakistani officers are far more the products of their institution than they are not. For confirmation, you present this theory to the Indian military attachés. They spend much time, on and off work, with their Pakistani counterparts and their word provides a stamp of authenticity.

While sources and undeveloped ideas are kept to oneself, personal interaction can still produce a mass of minor details that can slowly build up to a trove of understanding. Both sides know the game and I cannot minimize my gratitude to the Pakistani professionals who opened windows at my request or of their own volition.

~

Journalists keep such odd hours that most of our socializing involved fellow professionals. There were weddings, birthdays and other celebrations which we attended. With some we discovered other interests in common and through them met people from other fields. Nandini and I did not have a very wide social life in Islamabad, partly because it was quite a sleepy town and partly for the reason I keep alluding to and have yet to elaborate upon. Perhaps I could have explored more in Karachi or Lahore and I have no real excuse for not having done so.

To give an idea of the 'normal' life we led in Islamabad, it might be best to put out vignettes of my memories of the phases of the day. When writing about mornings it has to be about winter. Islamabad is roughly at the same latitude as Srinagar though much lower in altitude and the Margallas screen some of the bitter winds of the cold season. When the sun comes out to turn the white hoarfrost covering your lawn into so many rivulets, you really learn to appreciate the pleasure of a hot mug of coffee.

Traffic was light on the broad roads except during the very brief peak hours. It was never a hassle to drive out for an official assignment or attend a parliament session, especially since parking was never an issue. Shopping, whether for groceries, clothes or handicrafts involved a brief spin to one of the 'Supers'. These were shopping plazas rather than malls, which could have easily fitted in on the chic-range between Delhi's Sarojini and Khan markets. The difference was more in smells than sights since Balti or burger joints were more common than corner *tikki* stalls.

Nandini, as I have mentioned, taught at the Islamabad Grammar School run by Mrs Cheema, wife of a retired army officer. If I am not mistaken, the fact that she had taught at the Air Force School in Delhi's Subroto Park was a point in her favour when it came to the appointment. Nandini also took tuitions in English for the granddaughter of the lady who lived in the house just across.

Ramadan was of course the time when the markets would show their full riches and their contrasts. In the afternoons, the streets would be so quiet that even a non-Muslim could feel a little guilty as he walked to the *naan*-bakeries that never shut to pick up the slightly salted, delicious *rotis*. One thing I would notice as I passed each house on the way was that the scent of food on the fire would waft out even hours before Iftar at sunset.

Bakr Eid was the season when we filled our larder at no cost. The customary rule apparently was that the meat of a sacrificed goat had to be distributed to so many households and that of a heifer to so many more. The doorbell would ring again and again and every time you opened it, there would be someone with a saucerful of meat pieces. Once when I actually weighed the quantities given in a season it came to three kilos. To reciprocate, we would place orders for extra boxes when the High Commission sent vehicles to Amritsar to pick up sweets during Diwali.

Holi and Diwali were two days of the year when the Pakistanis seemed to cheerfully forget about Partition, especially the former. Once we four Indian correspondents, enjoying the festival of colour, were called to the Foreign Ministry for an urgent briefing at extremely short notice. None of us had the time to clean up and reached the Ministry with *gulal* splattered on faces and clothing. Not a single Pakistani batted an eyelid. If anything, they seemed envious. Years later, I believe, Nawaz Sharif declared Holi a national holiday. The scenes along Lahore's Canal Road must have been riotous.

Participation in Diwali, with its more pronounced Hindu connotations, was probably more problematic and I cannot remember any of our neighbours offering to light the *diyas*. All of them, as well as the ubiquitous intelligence men on the street, would make it a point to saunter past admiring the lights and pausing at the gate to accept sweets—but only if the *barfis* were from Amritsar! Perhaps the sole note of disappointment manifested on any of the festive occasions would be struck on the morning after Bakr Eid. Staff of the huge charity network run by Maulana Abdul Sattar Edhi would arrive in their pickup trucks to take away the hides households were only too happy to donate. Those poor *madrasa* boys just did not seem to be able to comprehend that there were non-Muslims who did not have a hide to offer.

Early evening was the time for the Margallas. It was one of the greatest joys of Islamabad and a really unique one. Imagine pulling up in a parking lot off the main road girdling a national capital, walking a few steps off the macadam and finding yourself in the wilderness. It was jungle and the clusters of boar in the clearings were not as harmless as those in Asterix comics. That did not deter hordes of people from hitting the trails and there were so many pathways that crowds could easily be avoided. For variety, you could drive up to Daman-e-Koh, a sort of picnic-pavilion that had more potential than successive lessees were able to extract. It was still a nice place to have tea and *pakodas* and it provided a magnificent view of the Potohar.

Evenings that were not spent at home or with friends, mostly from the High Commission, was Blue Area time. The main road in the city, which doubled as the city's Rajpath on Pakistan Day, had rows of commercial blocks set well back and away across flanking lawns. Most of these blocks had at least one up-scale restaurant—usually Chinese, Balti or northern Punjabi and soup never tasted so nice as it did after a winter evening spent walking around the sprawl of Takshashila. Or even vodka for that matter as we found out one evening when a group of young ladies sitting at an adjacent table insisted that we fill our glasses with the contents of the steel jugs on their table. It was a settled arrangement whereby they handed over the bottles on the quiet, the restaurant mixed in the water or juice and the company could sip in apparent innocence. Ah! The evil joys of privilege.

Jumma, the weekly holiday, usually opened with a trip to the bazaar for vegetable shopping and browsing through the curio stalls run by Afghan refugees. Apart from the rare artefacts that could startle you on occasion, the market also offered non-lethal by-products of the Afghan war. One of the pieces I picked up was a sniper scope that rattled about the drawers of the various desks I used at several homes before it disappeared in due course.

We usually returned from the Jumma Bazaar anticipating the fun of going through *Friday Times*. The tabloid-sized, broad-sheet quality publication always had interesting articles but Nandini and I vied to snatch up the back-pages, which featured satirical columns by the Mohsin sisters, Jugnu and Moni. The top of the page take-offs on political personalities as well as the biting commentary on social attitudes could keep us going for the rest of the week.

Four personalities—Ishaq Khan, Nawaz Sharif, Benazir and the then Sindh Chief Minister Jam Sadiq Ali—took turns on the top-of-the-page rip-offs each with an appropriate caricature. Benazir's was a Dear Diary piece written in convent English filled with the plaintive grievance-airing she had patented. Ishaq Khan wrote in bureaucratese and routinely under-lined certain sections or instructed that other parts be re-produced in triplicate.

Sharif probably got the rawest deal as he was depicted as a not too bright, provincial politician who was perpetually asking why people kept talking about killings and '*sara yeh woh*' (all this and that) in the same breath. The Balkans were on the boil at the time and Pakistan was continuously issuing statements condemning the killings in Sarajevo. Sharif's cartoon figure always had four hands, his own wrapped around his head and his ghost-writer's stuck through the armpits, holding the pen and pressing the paper. Jam Saab always appeared with a glass and cigar at hand and signed off with a 'tinkle, tinkle, sheers', the misspelling of cheers indicating that Jam Saab had imbibed a few already. Anyone puzzled by this allusion can jump to the Afterword where I offer some more details about Jam Sadiq Ali, one Pakistani politician who drank openly and did not give a damn for those who criticized him for it.

People who belong to the northern regions of the subcontinent are fortunate that they can make up for their cultural philistinism with their winter festivals. While the Urs of Bade Imam was the main folk event in those parts, the annual festival at Lok Virsa was the main national show-piece. Much in the manner of the India International Trade Fair it was a mix of the commercial and the cultural. Probably because of a more picturesque setting unmarred by architectural monstrosities, this fair seemed somewhat more authentic even though a preserve ultimately of the 'arty-farty' crowd.

The more interesting stalls were those that sold handicrafts: onyx ware, camel-skin lampshades, the full gamut of Kashmir curios, leather goods, handloom textiles, inlaid wood pieces and so on. Women liked to buy the exotic Kalash outfits from the Hunza Valley and I succumbed to the temptation of getting myself a Chitrali cap. This is the cap with the flat crown and curled brim that you see in pictures of Afghan warriors such as Ahmed Shah Massoud. Bought it and then buried it in the cupboard after learning the term western journalists had given it.

The lower, curled, part of the cap is actually an extension of the brim that is rolled up. Once unrolled, it covers the ears and provides nice warmth. However, because the centre of the cap is put on the head before the ends are rolled down, it closely resembles another male accessory and is therefore appropriately called the Condom Cap.

There was one piece of Pakistani handiwork so laden with irony that I found impossible to resist. Chiniot, a town close to Faisalabad, is famous for its gilt-inlaid furniture pieces. Among them is an ingeniously constructed bar that opens on top to reveal an extendable shelf on which you can keep your fancier bottles; looped slats on the insides for glasses; and a compartment at the bottom for extras. One such currently graces the space between the drawing and dining areas of my Kozhikode residence.

Food, as always, was the other major attraction of the Lok Virsa festival and in the time we were there, the Balochi 'Sajji' had pride of place. Somehow, I never came across any restaurant selling memorable Awadhi or Hyderabadi (Deccan as they specify in Pakistan) cuisine either at this festival or any of the cities but that might have been due to lapses on my side.

There would also be plenty of music and folk dancing with Nusrat Fateh Ali Khan, Abida Parveen and the band Junoon usually being the main features of the festival. Surprisingly, no special effort seemed to be made to promote classical music even though by some accounts, especially Wiki, Amir Khusro, considered the father of their national language, was also one of the first composers of the Hindustani tradition. No Dagar Bani, no equivalent of an Amjad Ali with his classical sarod, no one to follow in the footsteps of Vilayat Khan! For years, Seema Kirmani made valiant efforts to promote Kathak but Pakistanis seemed indifferent to this aspect of their cultural heritage as well.

One part of the festival grounds would be set aside for the martial arts. For some inexplicable reason, the wrestlers on display were always Sindhi. They were brawny, heavily muscled men alright but it seemed incongruous that the Punjabis had conceded the mud-pits to them. Perhaps it was because the Punjabis preferred to exhibit their sword skills.

A group of a dozen men would square off with wicker-work shields and canes for swords. They would go through the hops, whirls and spinning attacks of South Asian fencing which looks so different from the linear stylizations of the Western systems. Their *ustaad,* a wiry, sun-blackened Potohari could take on two or more at a time, trapping one opponent's sword arm under an armpit while slashing at the other two.

It was pretty good stuff. However, I would have bet then as I do now, that those Potoharis would not have lasted for very long against a Kalaripayattu maestro. Our Kerala style of sword play is the culmination of years of effort to make the body flexible, train the power to flow effortlessly, draw up the full force behind a blow and use blades with utter precision. A *Kalari abhyasi* develops so many angles and ways of cutting and thrusting by the time he finishes learning '*anka thaari*' (the combat mode) that even Kendo experts would be hard put to anticipate lines of attack.

As with classical music and dance, Pakistanis apparently did not want to come to terms with other aspects of their cultural heritage. Takshashila is less than an hour's drive from Islamabad and I lost count of the number of times I went there. It never failed to fascinate. This ancient Buddhist centre of learning is not one site but several spread over a number of hillsides. There are hardly any grand buildings left standing. Perhaps there never were because the foundation stones suggest a preference for architectural modesty. It is that very simplicity and the order and discipline that the whole complex conveys that constitutes the real beauty of the place.

To visit Takshashila on a winter evening with the golden sunlight giving way to mist and gloom is almost allegorical. You feel drawn into the glory of India, get saddened by its apparent eclipse and finally warmed by the joyful awareness that come the morning, Takshashila will still be there. How do you turn away from all that even if some ancestor along the line added on another stream of belief to your heritage?

A.H. Dani and other Pakistanis striving to preserve the remnants of the country's pre-Islamic heritage gave the impression of being beleaguered custodians. Funds did not seem to be the problem. To go by the general upkeep of the historic sites and the well-maintained appearance of the administrative buildings at these places, the federal government did not seem to stint on finances. The curse appeared to be one of benign indifference. 'We will provide the money because you and so many people in the world deem it important that we do,' the government seemed to be telling Dani and associates. 'But we are not really convinced that we need to do this.'

Dani, the doyen of Pakistani historians and archaeologists, very graciously presented me with a copy of his book on the Indus Valley on the first and only occasion that we met. It was very much in keeping with the broad-minded generosity expected from a person who was the first Muslim to get an MA in Sanskrit from Benares Hindu University. Perhaps it was my imagination but there seemed to be a further dimension to the gesture. Did Dani Saab present me with that book because he wanted evidence of his work to be preserved by the native of a country that better appreciated it?

A similar sense of poignancy scratched at the periphery of my mind when I first saw Moenjodaro. (This manner of spelling, which works out as a translation of the Sindhi term 'Mount of the Dead' seems a lot more appropriate than the usual rendering in our history textbooks. Besides, the Mohenjo Daro version instantly triggers an allusion to a distillery and that is hardly proper even though the cane-crushing facility is the source of the revered Old Monk.) If anything, the feeling of loss is even stronger since the site of this ancient trading city abuts onto the bank of the Indus to provide the reminder that its fate was linked to the state of the river. Those waters served as the life-line for centuries before turning into the cause of its demise. A super-flood, or alternatively a super-desiccation, theory are considered as presenting the most plausible explanation for the end of this civilization.

Nandini and I went to Moenjodaro at the height of the Sindh summer. If I remember right we took a reading of the thermometer outside the modest administrative block of the tourism or archaeological department and the mercury stood at 48 degrees Celsius. Apart from us the only other visitors were some Japanese tourists whose presence there had a pretty weird explanation. At some point along the ages, Buddhists built a stupa on the highest point, termed the Citadel in our text books. This singular feature has turned this Dravidian site into a stop-over in the global Buddhist-tourism circuit.

That the site is Dravidian hits home with shocking clarity when you step into the 'Great Bath' as they call the rectangular arena of dry earth with the ranks of steps leading down to it. It is a *kolam*, the bathing tanks that adjoin South Indian temples. I do not know whether it was this evidence of an ancestral link or the effect of over-powering heat that made me feel the lapping of water against my body when I stood in the bed of the tank and closed my eyes.

Moenjodaro's mystique is so very different from that of other ancient civilizational sites. About eight years later, I had the chance to visit Nineveh and Babylon, centres of civilizations that were contemporaneous to and had links with the Indus Valley. At those two sites in southern Iraq, mud walls with blue-tile frescoes of winged beasts stood in stark contrast to the palm trees and sand dunes of present-day Mesopotamia. However, it was clearly reconstruction work, not restoration, incapable of shaking off artificiality.

Egypt offers monuments of imposing scale and perhaps even greater antiquity. To see the Sphinx and its cluster of pyramids at Gizeh, the massive pillars, walls and statues of Luxor or the elegant temple of Hatshepsut is to marvel at the grand vision and mighty effort that made such monuments possible. Moenjodaro provides a counter-point since the civilizational aspiration here had a different orientation.

To see the houses constructed with the aim of maximizing sunlight, shade and ventilation, the dead straight streets with drainage of matching quality, and provision for indoor plumbing is to appreciate the human-centred idea of development that our ancients bequeathed to us. Engineering of such perfection that the centuries have barely moved bricks out of alignment. Construction dedicated not to the gods or god-kings but to the welfare of the common citizen. It is this aim, reflected in every inch of this Indus Valley city that instils pride in a rich heritage.

As in other parts of the subcontinent, civic service in about 2000 CE did not match that of 2000 BCE. There were no guides with real expertise available and the signposts were few and not very informative. Nandini and I dredged our memories to salvage lessons from long-forgotten textbooks until an Arya-descended gardener saw us pottering around and came over to guide us. He knew all the architectural tricks of the place—the hatchways that could be lifted to draw water from underground channels, ingenious grain stores and so on. His was a very conscientious assistance with none of his considerable knowledge held back.

Still, I do not think he should have gone so far as to demonstrate how my ancestors, not his, evacuated their bowels into the drains under their homes.

Encrusting Enmity

If I had thought that I had leached the last drop of sweat in my body into the hot earth of Moenjodaro, I could not have been more wrong. Pakistan's intelligence services made me realize that there were gallons of perspiration still inside. That summer day was one of the worst of my tenure though there were quite a few others.

We had finished our round of the Indus Valley site, drunk several bottles of water each and taken an auto to Larkana airport hoping to find some food in the terminal. We did not get anything to eat. Only a belly-full of real desperation. I had booked our tickets through a travel agent in Karachi, had encountered no trouble on the way in and was absolutely nonchalant when I handed the vouchers across the counter for the return flight. The man did the usual checks and told me that we were not booked on the flight. By then I had spent most of my three-year tenure and my mental alarms went off at top decibels.

In those days, probably now as well, 'Indian spies' were routinely apprehended in rural Sindh, all of them ostensibly on missions to provoke rebellion. Some were 'shot while attempting to escape' and were probably the lucky ones since the fate of those captured does not bear thinking about. Now here we were, an Indian couple in interior Sindh, with non-diplomatic passports and an alibi that could be torn to shreds.

I also knew by then that the Punjab Police Special Branch, the federal Intelligence Bureau and ISI knew about me and that the knowledge had not pleased them. A friend or two in the High Commission was aware that we had planned the trip but had few other details and a twenty-four- or forty-eight-hour gap between our last contact and the appearance of our mugshots in the newspapers or TV screens would not lead anyone to take notice until it was too late. Those were of course pre-mobile days and trunk lines were not very reliable even if we were allowed to use them.

Sweat burst from every pore. I had bungled horribly and put Nandini and self in terrible danger. Desperate, I asked the PIA staff if there was any other way I could reach Karachi. Bus was the only other option and that was not a choice at all. Indians traversing Sindh from one end to the other offered an even more suspect profile than if they were stuck in Larkana. There was nothing else to do other than lay out the facts for the PIA man and underscore that he would share guilt for our deaths or torture if he did not put us on the plane.

Airlines officials pointed me towards the man in white Awami lurking inside and said that he was the only one who could decide. I went in, told him that I had after all got special permission for making the trips and that there was no call for holding us back. He sized me up very coolly, told me to wait outside and casually reached for the phone. With that approach I had blown whatever faint chance there was to sneak off to the bus stand. After agonizingly long minutes Awamiman told PIA to not just put us on the manifest but also load us in as soon as the shuttle from Karachi landed and emptied.

Relief was so profound that my brain barely registered a very important political development that took place moments later. From my window seat I could make out that our plane was not being cleared for take-off though the tugs had been removed. Then another aircraft, smaller and marked in some other colours than the PIA's taxied to a parallel bay and parked. A few cars drew up, a few people including a tall lady in a white dupatta moved quickly from the vehicles to the plane which promptly shut its doors and took off.

By then I had seen enough of Benazir in parliament house, leading processions, speaking at rallies and addressing press conferences to be able to identify the lady in the white *dupatta*. With that the rest of the story began to fall into place. Benazir had been under house arrest in Larkana while the caretaker government led by Moeen Qureshi tried to put Pakistan's house—especially its economy—in order. A few weeks earlier, the establishment—which by then essentially meant General Waheed Kakar and his colleagues in the Corps Commanders Conference—had sent Ishaq Khan and Sharif packing.

Although a military action it was not really resented on account of the universal recognition that there was a huge mess that had to be cleaned up. An integral part of the clean-up was the promise that elections would be held and power transferred to the winner once Qureshi had finished his work. There had been much speculation about the time-frame and the sight of the white lady boarding a mysterious plane could be interpreted in two ways. She was either being shifted to another place of detention or being summoned for talks.

Without any knowledge of Benazir's destination, I really had no story. It took a day or so for the Pakistani media to work its way through the back-room manoeuvres and report that Benazir as well as Sharif would be allowed to contest. All I got out of my experience and the mental torture undergone was certitude about the authenticity of the story once it came out.

To spin off from my experience with the intelligence men to an exposition of the political games of the time might seem like a diversion. It really is not because there is a connection.

While a high-stakes game was going on, the authorities probably did not want to simultaneously deal with a bilateral, possibly international, rumpus consequent on the manhandling of a foreign correspondent. They had sent a jolt of fear through me and were apparently well satisfied.

~

Was I in a state of paranoia then or now? Only those Indians who have lived in Pakistan for a length of time will understand the truth of the matter. As far as others are concerned, I would like to offer some facts and some scenarios so that they can judge for themselves.

A first fact, irrefutable and unavoidable, is that an Indian living in Pakistan is under surveillance twenty-four-seven. Phones are tapped—there might be a few bugs in your house depending on your importance—and there are watchers in shifts of two men apiece outside your house at all times. (Pakistanis living in India probably suffered the same attention but their troubles do not register when you have enough of your own.) Sometimes our car-or-motorcycle-riding 'followers' would come up to say that they were keeping tabs 'for your safety' ('*Aapki hifazat ke liye*') and would then belie their words by closing to within inches of your bumper or boring headlights into the rear-view mirror.

Nandini flew into Karachi from Mumbai a couple of months after I set up shop and I went down to receive her. That whole night, every five minutes or so, the phone in our hotel room rang long enough to jerk us out of whatever sleep we could snatch before cutting off. Pure, cheap harassment, as if to tell us that they could disrupt conjugal bliss at any moment they chose. Over time you come to realize that the message is actually more sinister.

Your wife goes out, promising to return by 6.30 in the evening. By 6.45, if there is no sign of her, you are fighting the itch to go and wait for her on the road outside or to file a missing person report with the High Commission. It is not a laughing matter. There have been cases where the wives of Indian personnel have been deliberately harassed in order to send a message to their husbands. Or a Pakistani lady has gone through an unpleasant experience in Delhi, the report has flashed back to her husband's colleagues and they have initiated retaliation before the parallel Indian chain gets activated. You and your family can suffer for some act committed by some unknown person or agency in Delhi.

Men assigned to cover you for two or three months at a time can become friendly over that period. A mention has already been made about the inspector level gent who asked me to join him for tea. On another occasion, when I went to the airport to receive the person who succeeded me, I suddenly found a hand closing in on the far-side grip of the suitcase that I was lugging from the trolley to the car and found that it was one of my 'followers'. They would also come up for brief chats when you were waiting for someone and could be really helpful when you were trying to locate a new address. On the whole, however, their attentions were certainly not welcome.

The system was built to ensure animosity. We journalists were low enough in the pecking order to not merit full-time attention from any force more powerful than the Punjab Police Special Branch. There were High Commission officials who were under surveillance by the Intelligence Bureau and that organization's loop was wide enough to cover us en passant. The three defence attachés were followed by the intelligence units of their respective mirror services and the whole shebang was kept on its toes by the ISI. So much so that the Punjab policemen following us seemed to be in fear of being pulled up by the big brother if they did not display sufficient rigour.

If we of the 'officer class' were under constant pressure, it was as nothing compared to the plight of the clerical, security and ministerial staff of the High Commission. They were often pushed to the very edge, just short of actual physical force. What can a lone employee of the High Commission do when he is ringed by a dozen louts during the short walk to the nearby bank? Any kind of retaliation is foolhardy because the foreigner, especially the 'foreign enemy', will invariably be the ultimate loser.

The psychological strain imposed on proud men forced to restrain themselves while being humiliated in such a way is unconscionable. Can there be any wonder that the rest of us had such high regard for the officers who could take on the thugs and did? During my time in Islamabad, we were lucky to have two very tough High Commissioners—Dixit and S.K. Lambah with M.K. Bhadrakumar as chargé d'affaires in between. We also had our 'Kapoor Saab'—Rajeev Kapoor—and the defence attachés. Of the latter, I have already mentioned Maj Gen Duggal. Before him, there was Brigadier Raizada who had served in a unit that had closed in on Lahore during the '65 war. He loved to tell the Pakistanis, 'I had the heart of your country in my fist and could have squeezed it at will.'

Then there was Anil Bakshi. Our naval attaché loved to run. On the roads in the city, his followers could chase him on their bikes. Anil would take them for a run on the hill trails of the Margallas, leaving green-faced intelligence personnel gasping in his wake. They tried bumper-riding his car; Anil braked, the follower got his fender dented and tried to put up a brave show by telling our sailor not to think of picking a fight since all the men around him were Muslims. 'Don't talk to me about Muslims,' Anil shoots back, 'We have more Muslims in our country than you have here.'

Incidents of this sort stand out in bold relief with the

passage of years and so mute the feelings that it is difficult to re-experience the tension which gripped you at that time. It was constant, relentless and unsparing when push came to shove. If you got on the wrong side of the agencies, the Commission would probably be able to save you from execution or long imprisonment but not from expulsion. Other embassies, including the champions of liberty, would abruptly discover that the Indo-Pak imbroglio was beyond the ambit of standard norms. Foreign correspondents, taking the cue from their embassies, would treat you likewise and the local media knew that they were helpless. In the blink of an eye the world could turn into a small Indian island surrounded by a hostile sea.

Such became the case in the summer of 1992 though I was far from being the main victim. My mother and my in-laws, visiting together, landed in Lahore and we had gone to receive them. We had booked into Falettis, the iconic hotel, for a variety of reasons. Falettis was the Metro-Goldwyn-Meyer team's base during the shooting of the Ava Gardner/Stewart Granger starrer *Bhowani Junction* and some of the scenes might have been shot there as well. The book from which the screenplay was adapted was written by John Masters who served in 2/4 Gorkha Rifles and Bhowani is the name he gave to Jabalpur (the locale for this novel as well as *Nightrunners of Bengal*). Nandini and family had lived in Jabalpur when her father was at the Signals School and therefore the connection could not be missed.

A second reason was that Falettis was one of the few hotels in Lahore that had a permit room. With the hotel granted this concession, I as a non-Muslim could buy liquor from the in-house storeroom and would not need to carry a bottle from Islamabad. After a hectic day visiting Lahore Fort, Kim's gun and other tourist attractions in the city, Nandini's father and I had just finished our baths and charged our glasses when the hazy Doordarshan telecast (it could be received in Lahore) spewed out shocking news.

A senior officer in the High Commission, Rakesh Mittal, had been abducted and tortured by Pakistani intelligence outfits, was the news from India. On switching channels we finally got the report from the directly opposite angle. According to Pakistan TV, an official of the High Commission had been apprehended when he was collecting confidential material from a source and was injured while resisting arrest. There was nothing that could be done that night or on the way next day as we returned to Islamabad with storm clouds of apprehension building up against the effort to stay calm.

After paying off the taxi, as I was hauling the luggage to the doorway, I noticed that the drawing room air-conditioner had been ripped out of its knee-high niche and was lying on the ground. A quick unlock and look around showed that the colour TV and VCR were missing. I called up Rajeev for advice and he told me to report the theft to the police station near the Shah Faisal mosque and then come back home and sit tight. He would be along shortly.

At the station the uniformed men were very polite and also very helpless. 'You are an Indian aren't you,' they asked. 'Yes! I am,' I replied. You are under surveillance are you not, was the next question. Affirmative once again. Sighs all round. 'We cannot help you. Better ask them.' The policemen were actually sympathetic.

Rajeev filled me in on the rest. Mittal and family had come to my house for dinner a few days earlier. There had been a small misunderstanding about time and I was waiting at the gate to ask my guests to excuse me for a few minutes since I needed to get cigarettes. Rakesh too had to go to the market for something and so he dropped off Mrs Mittal and I got into the car. We reached the supermarket, Rakesh went one way, I another and we were both back in the car in very short order.

His followers had got wrong-footed when we split and they were apparently convinced that I had served as a decoy for whatever my friend had been up to. Rakesh was picked up outside his house a few days later, taken to some secret locale, beaten badly and subjected to electric shocks. The questions had covered the whole gamut and among them were queries related to my role that night and about my supposed service for Indian intelligence. Rakesh did not give them any satisfaction on questions pertaining to either himself or me.

To say that I was on hyper-alert for the next few days is no exaggeration. Over the course of the week, Rakesh and family left, the situation seemed to be settling and we took our parents for a tour of Takshashila. As I have mentioned earlier, the historic site is not a single one but a composite of three or more and you have to drive from one to the other. We were on our way from the second to the third when I noticed that there was a real swarm of intelligence men about. They were generally physically fit people wearing Awami of different shades of brown and their occupation was obvious even without uniform. If further confirmation was needed, I found it in the form of a field telegraph unit set up under a canvas awning by the roadside.

I felt calm. A thorough beating at least seemed very much on the cards but I had a feeling that the others in the car with me would be spared. There was no logic to back up this conclusion and it was probably wishful thinking more than anything else. Although, to be fair, Pakistanis do observe restraint up to a point when it comes to '*buzurgs*' and '*khawateens*'. Or, perhaps, I had begun to mentally prepare myself. A high pain threshold would not ultimately be enough and my main worry was about how long I would last before shaming myself in the eyes of my tormentors or my own.

Meanwhile, Lt Col (retd.) M. Sathesan of the Indian Army's Corps of Signals, sitting in the front passenger seat, had recognized fellow *faujis* even though they were in civvies. His officer spirit took over, head tilted up, face set in proud lines and he gave them the inspection they seemed to be asking for. That, I am convinced, served as my first line of defence. An aura of command was radiating so strongly from the good Colonel, that the Pakistani majors and JCOs felt compelled to hold back.

It would not have held them back for very much longer. For that to happen—as it finally did—there would need to have been some singing of the wires between the field staff, IB or ISI offices, the Foreign Ministry, the Press Information Department and perhaps the Prime Minister's office until a decision to abort the exercise was taken. From all of the above, it must not be thought that I had suddenly acquired

VIP status. That was just standard operating procedure. How do I know that?

~

My tenure ended a year later and it appeared likely that I would not get another twelve-month extension on my visa. That was too bad because the political crisis involving Sharif and Ishaq Khan was reaching breaking point and I wanted desperately to cover it. My bosses, especially Malini Parthasarathy, who was Executive Editor at the time and a keen follower of Pakistan developments, threw their full weight behind the efforts to convince my hosts. It looked like a losing battle and I had started off on the rounds of farewell meals when I got a several-times re-routed message that I should at the soonest call Shafqat Khakakhel who was in charge of the India desk in the Foreign Ministry.

'Where the fuck have you been?' was the first exasperated comment from Shafqat when I finally got through to him. He sounded quite irritated by the need to chase me around town so I refrained from retorting that I had been stuffing myself since his government had left me no choice. The gist of his message was that I should go to the relevant office with my passport in order to get the visa stamped on it. When I went to thank Shafqat, I asked him how the turnaround had come about.

'It was initially refused at the highest level but I went there and argued for you,' was his reply.

'At the highest level? Surely Ishaq Khan can't be bothered about my whereabouts,' I said in an attempt at witticism.

'No! The level just below that,' Shafqat said seriously. That meant Nawaz Sharif. A moment of self-flattery that my case had gone so high gave way immediately to the realization that the India angle was too important for even the prime minister to attend to minor details. And that is the root of the problem. The state is so highly sensitized about its dealings with India that its full weight is brought to bear even on problems that can be dealt with at departmental levels.

Shafqat himself did not hide his disgust at the sheer bloody-mindedness that could be on display. He once told me about the reports that the intelligence services would submit about the movements of Indian diplomats.

'I have to keep pointing out that the reports are useless since I was at most of these bloody parties myself.'

Shafqat and Mubarak Shah, for some time the head of the Press Information Department, had both served in the Pakistan High Commission in India. They had cultivated a sardonic attitude towards the whole surveillance business. Mubarak had a lovely way of dealing with the powers above as well as me. Every now and then he would call me up and chat about some innocuous subject. Then deliver his punchline, which was something more than a message yet far from amounting to a threat.

'Yaar. Haath thoda dheela kar.' (Literally: Friend. Loosen your hand a little. Implicitly: soften your reporting.)

People like Shafqat and Mubarak made dealings with Pakistani officialdom manageable even if not completely pleasant. Arguably, their approach was also more effective since they let you know when you were veering close to the edge. This was fair warning. Harsher criticism of my work might have prodded me to working on ways to insert another kick into my next report. Quite in contrast was another officer in the PID who was ostensibly next-in-rank to Mubarak though he had the smell of the intelligence services all over him.

This man called me to the Central Secretariat one Thursday afternoon soon after taking up his post. It was supposed to be a courtesy call but as I began to traverse the endless empty corridors on the way to his office, I could not help speculating that it would be very easy to abduct and throw me into a cell if someone so wanted. While that did not happen, this official kept muttering beneath his breath and making indecipherable allusions to show that he did not care very much for India or Indians. The man did not seem to realize that he was coming across as being too pathetic to do anything about his feelings.

Hostility from the top got multiplied several fold down the line. Active personnel of the intelligence services never got physical with me. A couple of *lifafas* did, however, and in identical fashion and at the same venue—the press office in the parliament building. This was a smallish room on the floor above the main legislative halls and not much frequented. On both occasions, the *lifafa* concerned, seeing me approach, turned back to the man at the desk as if he had remembered something.

Then, just as I came parallel to the point of their shoulders Lifafa 1, and many days later, Lifafa 2 spun around swinging right hands out to smash into my throat. Apparently accidents, done on purpose. Lifafa 1 was a short man who had to reach a little high and I could smother the blow by tucking my chin and twisting my shoulder into its path. Lifafa 2 was taller than me and reputedly had been a boxer in his youth. His backhander went right home.

That was when I came to know that the spirit of *satyagraha* had seeped into my lizard brain. There is no point in fighting in these circumstances because you can only get into deeper trouble with greater numbers. Flight, or surrender to the pain, which is the same thing, was not an option either. Instinct took over. I managed to avoid a break in my stride. My throat muscles worked through a swallow to ease the pain and I was able to ask the PID man for some papers in a normal voice. The look of utter bafflement on the *lifafa*'s face provided for far greater elation than any counter-punch could have. It was while I was reflecting on the incident later that I truly appreciated what a tactical genius the Mahatma was.

A turning of the other cheek was not an option available to the non-officer cadre at the High Commission. If they did, their tormentors were certain to double down. Provocations would continue until our man lost his cool, but then what could he do against a dozen opponents or more. Even if he turned out to be Bruce Lee in disguise the downward spiral would continue with his being dubbed an agent provocateur to begin with before the machinery slowly ground him to pulp. It was a slow suffocation of self-respect.

Other than the incidents set out above, the only other 'physical' move against me occurred on the night of 6 December 1992. We returned home after dark and found that someone had used a football-sized boulder to smash a gash through our front door. Whether it was the hand of the 'followers' or that of some neighbour genuinely incensed over the demolition of the Babri Masjid on that day was impossible to ascertain.

Actually, the authorities did take care of those of us who could have been targets of fanatics. A special police agent was assigned for guard duty at our house. He commandeered a chair and sat in the front porch until a sudden downpour brought about the sharp drop in temperature that could sometimes happen in Islamabad. Then he joined us inside sipping tea and watching me go through endless newspaper articles. After a couple of hours of this bodyguard routine we both concluded that another door-smashing was not on the cards. He seemed quite happy about the early end to his duty.

There were hardly any reports in the Pakistan media of Hindus being attacked in retaliation. Such reports as came in our own media mentioned incidents in places from where it was not possible to get verification. We, Indian journalists, came to know about one temple being vandalized in Rawalpindi only because the authorities invited us to see the restoration work they had undertaken. It was a fairly unconvincing episode.

The 'temple' building did have some 'Hindu' features adorning the front parapet of the terrace. That in itself did not mean anything since there were buildings in the older quarters of this and other towns that had the same kind of decorations. Almost as if the Muslims who moved in after the Hindus left in or after 1947 had been so busy changing the interiors to their convenience that they had not bothered about a few harmless filigrees on the facade. This was also not a standalone temple like Katas Raj or Hasan Abdal. It was part of a row of houses and posed a special problem for me.

In same manner as most Malayali Hindus, I sometimes find it difficult to treat seriously temples beyond the Western Ghats. Okay! Kshetras in Dakshin Kanara, the Thalakaveri shrine and the major pilgrimage centres such as Kashi Vishwanath are exceptions. Temples elsewhere, as far as we are concerned, cannot come close to matching the sanctity of even our local shrines, leave alone Guruvayur. So, I could not see this Pindi place of worship as a spot where I would offer prayers. The *pujari*, or the person who passed for one, was in Awami, kept his thread hidden if he did have one and seemed to be looking at us to give him instructions.

Later, I was to get flak from colleagues in India for not reporting on the destruction of temples in Pakistan. This did not leave me hurt so much as bewildered. Had my critics forgotten Partition? There are no Hindus in the parts of Pakistan my visa stipulations allowed me to visit and therefore no functioning temples either, I wanted to tell them. Hasan Abdal and presumably Katas Raj were kept going by Hindu/Sikhs from the Seraiki region or Sindh, where Partition-era killings had not reached genocidal proportions.

In point of fact, Pakistani Muslims who (in '92) attacked buildings that were once temples seemed to be hurting themselves more than anyone else. Quite a few of these buildings have been converted to libraries or *madrasas* or charity clinics and quite consciously so. In Jhelum and Chakwal, if I remember right, people who ran these institutions told me that the buildings had been deliberately re-purposed in this way so that their aura of venerability would not be totally eroded. Although they were no longer centres of worship, they would continue to be treated with respect.

At least some among the post-Partition generation seemed to have let curiosity replace religious hatred. It was raining incessantly during my one visit to Hasan Abdal (Gurudwara Panja Sahib) for the annual festival. Water was running every which way, over plates of *gulal*, through the rice and *dal* of the *langar* and squelching marigold into the pathways. The whole was a near nauseating mess and I felt myself squirming with embarrassment when the young District Management Officer, equivalent to possibly an Assistant Collector of ours, came to stand alongside me.

I half expected a scornful sniff and even a comment on how Islam managed such affairs better. What I got was nothing of the sort. After a long inspection of the Hindu/Sikhs from the Seraiki and Sindh going about their rituals not in the least concerned about the rain, he turned to me and said with deep respect, 'Religion can really raise people up can't it? Look at them, totally unmindful of their difficulties.'

That administrator was not a rarity but there were not many exceptions like him. Liberal Pakistanis, the types we mostly mixed with, did not wear their religion on their sleeves, could joke about some of their beliefs and practices and had strong distaste for mullahs. Even then, religiosity and the Islamic fervour of that time was so much in the air that it was impossible to discount the impression that a majority considered people of other faiths as being deprived in some respect.

Then there were the mullah hordes and their enablers among those who posed as liberals. The supineness of the last-mentioned category was contemptible. They knew that the fanatics were promoting a brand of the religion that was barbaric, inhumane and against their (the liberals') own interest as well as their understanding of the tenets. Yet, they would set out to laud the frothy-mouthed for being pious. So much so that they would crowd-scream the true liberals into silence. As mentioned earlier, a person did not have to be a non-Muslim or an Ahmadiyya to invite the ire of the fanatics.

One weekday, I was going somewhere with the Three Old Men. At one particular junction, Rizvi Saab in the front passenger seat told Naqvi, who was driving, to turn away from the direct route. When the three of us made our surprise evident, Rizvi muttered that a meeting was being held at a Sunni mosque that was notorious for the fanaticism of its attendees. Three prominent Shias driving by their front-door would have been too tempting for them to resist. At that time, an extremist Sunni outfit called the Sipah-e-Sahaba was well into its murderous campaign against the followers of Ali.

That episode was one of those that opened my eyes to the plight of people living through a period of time when a creed hostile to them was well on its way towards asserting dominance. During a visit to Thatta in Sindh, Nandini and I were given an idea of how much more harrowing life can be when the pressure is building by the day and all around. We had spent most of the day with an extended Memon family and a couple among them took us over to meet their Hindu acquaintances.

They did not seem to be friends. The Hindus were too suspicious and the Memons too defensive for their relationship to be at a level above cool formality. Our hosts took us from the end of their part of the village across about fifty metres of open ground to what we initially assumed was another block of buildings. A few men sitting on plastic garden chairs watched us approach with no hint of warmth. There was a tenseness between the two groups that was not eased by our Muslim hosts' explanation that we were Indians who had come to learn about life in Sindh. In fact, the discomfort was so palpable that the Memons withdrew after requesting the Hindus to show us the way back once we had finished.

One of the younger men immediately asked Nandini to accompany him to the lady's quarters. A cup and saucer were brought out and we conversed while sipping tea. As the discussions went on I could see that they were trying to draw information out of me while basically stonewalling my enquiries. My subconscious mind also registered another fact that came into focus and became significant only a little later. Young men took turns to leave the tea-sipping session only to appear a little later whereupon another young man would get up and leave.

It was dark by the time the session ended and the men slow-walked me to another point along the block where Nandini suddenly exited from a door and plonked down in front of me. At this juncture, the men pointed the way and hastily withdrew. Nandini looked totally nonplussed. If my session with the men had been quite strange, her encounters with the women had been bizarre.

She had been led in through the door of what she assumed was one house. There the womenfolk had asked her some questions, then led her to an opening in a wall that led into what seemed like another house. More questions, then through an opening into yet another dwelling. It was as if she had entered a maze and she was thoroughly disoriented by the time she was let out of a last door and found me waiting for her.

She had noticed young men leaving the venues of each session just as she entered. We compared notes and discovered that the whole community had been doing the very same thing. After listening to my answers the young men were going indoors to tell the womenfolk to ask Nandini the same questions, trying to ascertain whether our versions matched. For the two of us it was a weirdly unsettling experience. For a minority community that was constantly in a state of siege, it was a well-thought out and practiced survival procedure.

Revanchist feelings did crop up in my mind after I left Pakistan, especially in the first few months. But I only had to flip the picture around to find a cure. Muslims, Dalits and some other communities in India have undoubtedly experienced a similar dread, an apprehension of imminent persecution, from time to time. Have they felt the same sort of constant oppression that minorities in Pakistan have to put up with? I do not think so. If, however, some of our countrymen believe with valid reason that their situation is the same as that of minorities in Pakistan, our nation will be a lot less than I think it is.

International public opinion is nowhere near as agitated as it needs to be over the discrimination faced by Hindus, Sikhs and Christians in Pakistan. That lacuna has to be addressed. But it is not if our approach is to attack Muslims here for what their co-religionists are doing to minorities elsewhere. Oppression of the innocent is cowardly and despicable no matter what the cause.

A subliminal dread never leaves the Indian living in Pakistan. Notions about all that can possibly go wrong are automatically processed out of the forefront of the mind as you go about your life and work and you are not even aware of the tension inside. It lies there, constantly exerting an unspecific pressure. Metaphorically, it is akin to undigested food pressing against the diaphragm.

On the last day, an hour or so into our drive from Islamabad to Amritsar, I saw the 'follower's' car behind me flashing its headlights. Soon it started tooting its horn. I slowed down, wondering whether the intelligence services had prepared a nasty farewell present and bracing myself for what was to come. The white car drew parallel, the inhabitants waved to me, drew back and pulled into a U-turn. Only then did I realize that we had crossed the Pindi division border and out of the jurisdiction of my usual complement.

Still, it was only after we had driven through the gates of the Wagah checkpost, shedding the Pakistani number plates on the way, that I had the sensation usually experienced when exiting the PIA plane in Delhi, of a weight being lifted off my shoulders.

Right at this juncture, when remembering the lightness felt on returning to India, my mind reconnected with a very important aspect of my life in Pakistan. It was like my mental processes had been brought back on line in the same manner as a rail track near the platform is yanked into alignment with the throughway by the pulling of a lever. I had earlier spoken about an alienation of a degree deeper than any felt in other unfamiliar situations. A feeling that was of a different order from the lack of connect initially experienced on going to our Punjab or Kashmir.

I was in Srinagar when the ongoing thirty-plus years of unrest first broke out in April 1989, making me one of the first non-resident journalists to start covering it. State police officials had told me that youth organizations in the State, armed and trained by Pakistan, were about to create major trouble. Even before the flare-up occurred they had hinted that whatever was to come would probably be worse than anything seen since the accession. *The Hindu/Frontline/Sportstar* photographer V.V. Krishnan (the person who took the snap of Jonty Rhodes flying through the air to effectuate a run out) and I were in one of the inner-city localities—Habbakadal if I remember right—when the thin-metal tack-tack-tack of an AK-47 on full automatic served as the first confirmation of confidential police briefings. We were escorted out of the locality by a group of youngsters who made no secret of their sympathies and might have been armed themselves.

Before that, for three to four years, I had travelled to Punjab every two or three months to cover the second phase of the Khalistan movement. Although I missed Black

Thunder (being in Kerala at that time because my father had passed away), I had been into Khalistani-held territory, including the Harmandir Sahib, routinely. In the course of the job, I had been introduced to the crack-thud sequence that signified shots fired towards me in anger. There had been meetings with dacoits and forays into Naxalite-infested Bastar earlier in my career.

None of those experiences had left me with the sense of helplessness that sometimes hit with tidal wave force while living in Pakistan. Perhaps the apposite word is not helplessness because you have to hold firm to your wits and your will for as long as you can. The operative word would actually be 'supportlessness' if the English lexicon permits such liberties. You are suddenly deprived of all support systems other than the High Commission and our diplomats can pull you to safety only if and to the extent they are allowed.

To be made to suddenly feel that you are stranded in a small Indian island in a hostile sea was only the start. The island too is a virtual entity until you reach it and obtain sanctuary. In India, you have the confidence that you can rely on family, friends and the authorities to help you when you are in trouble. As a journalist you get accustomed to being given friendly treatment by politicians and bureaucrats. Your status as a citizen of a democratic country makes you feel entitled to certain protections and civic society institutions do kick in more often than not to aid you.

None of that applies if you are an Indian in Pakistan. Every single layer of protection can be stripped away on the instant since even our diplomats have sometimes found that immunities can be withdrawn without warning. Senior officials of the Foreign Ministry respected my work and I had the goodwill of political leaders from a fairly broad spectrum. All that would have meant nothing at the crunch. Pakistani civic society, media and even well-placed friends cannot assist you because you have become highly toxic to them. They will be in as deep trouble if they lift a finger. Some have suggested that Pakistanis in India are identically placed. However, there is a difference in that more firmly entrenched democratic and rule of law traditions do provide a degree of protection.

Here then is the answer to that implicit question whether there is something unique to the Pakistani national mindset that sets them apart from the rest of humanity as far as Indians are concerned. The answer is that Pakistan marks an Indian as a person apart. It suits the establishment's interests to so mark you and years of propaganda and our own misdeeds have concretized that characterization. In our Punjab during the Khalistan period and even in Kashmir, at least in the early phase, the danger was generic. In Pakistan the threat can become direct and personal.

How this has come about is essentially background noise. What is fundamental is that you have been designated an enemy well before you enter Pakistan; even though you may never go anywhere near the place. Inside the country, there are multiple agencies working to ensure that people treat you like one. However, they cannot entirely prevent the calling out of a common humanity or quell the natural impulse of the ordinary citizen to deal with you normally. Caught in the middle, you feel the strength of both waves. As with life in general, the best you can do is hold on to the positives while taking the negatives in your stride.

Afterword

Most of the events narrated in this book unfolded around thirty years ago. My objective in recounting them was to not merely provide an idea of what Pakistan was like at that time. A further intent was to use those anecdotes as illustrations of traits I believe endure to the present day. In response to this assertion, a reader would have full justification for asking, 'How do you know? You've not been there since '93!'

Well! Many people write about Pakistan without having stepped onto its territory even once. Or after spending such short stints there that they do not really get a feel of the place. Still, a one-time familiarity might be seen as conferring an advantage so slight as to be dismissible. So here are two further factors I adduce in support of my claim that this book has some utility. Firstly, I never stopped following Pakistani affairs and writing about them, so the thirty years have been filled by a body of work, not a vacuum. Secondly, others who are au courant with the situation there, do acknowledge that I have something relevant to say about recent developments.

From what I have followed in the Pakistani media, one

significant change that has apparently taken place since I was there is the expansion of the middle class. Such a class did exist in the 1990s and its presence was very evident in the metropolises, Lahore and Karachi. Opinion-propounders were almost all from this class, as they often are, and they reflected the range from the far right to the left (but not too far left) of centre. Among them were staunch champions of human rights, democracy and independence in foreign policy with a noticeably smaller number of outspoken secularists. Their critiques were also directed, perhaps not strongly enough, against the feudal and business elites, which more or less monopolized electoral politics. Unforgivably, the articulate class also contained large numbers of ideological warriors for the anti-democratic institutions, the military and mullahdom. All these writers put together represented a segment of society that lacked real political clout and served mainly to vent prevailing moods. Today, the claim is that this class has begun to wield real influence.

Although I have not got my hands on any study that details the change in size or relevance of this class, media reports do provide some pointers. Broadly, the expansion appears to have followed the same pattern as it did in India and occurred due to similar causes. The information technology revolution has led to the creation of new forms of employment and a general enhancement in incomes, albeit on a smaller scale than in India. Income level is, of course, the most appropriate factor to be taken into consideration in attempting to define this segment of society and thus measure its size. As we have learned from our own experience, however, the demarcation line gets very hazy at the bottom edge. People at the lower end might actually be getting more money than they were earlier but rise in the cost of living and so on might have whittled down the worth of their earnings. Statistics, official or otherwise, can be highly suspect since public administrators and market managers have each their reasons to inflate the size of this segment.

Occupations seem to offer another factor for demarcating the contours of this class. So long as a person is not an agrarian or business magnate on the one hand or a wage labourer on the other, a slot can be reserved for him or her in the middle ranks. Here again, the lines can be very blurry indeed. A person who is otherwise a landless rural worker might open a cycle repair shop or sell peanuts from a pushcart. Is such a person a worker, an artisan or a petty businessman? People involved in these occupations could ply the same trade in towns, village *mandis* or even fairly busy highway bus stops. So, the place in which they operate might not be a strong enough indicator of their class. A few chosen *paanwallahs* in Delhi or Mumbai (possibly Karachi or Lahore for that matter) make more money than an average doctor or lawyer in mofussil towns, skewing the concept of a middle class even further.

With the advent of mechanized farming and burgeoning of commercial agriculture, widening scope for agro-businesses, improvements in transportation, spread of urban facilities and tastes to rural areas and so on, the sub-continental *dehat* is no longer what it once was. As has happened in large swathes of India, labour migration has impacted pockets of Pakistan in major ways. Workers from Khyber Pakhtunkhwa and POK have been ubiquitous in the Gulf and further afield since the 1970s at least. But the impact they have made on their societies, substantial though it is, would surely be less marked than the effect Punjabi workers have had on theirs. With cash in hand, shrewder peasants look for other ways to increase their wealth and all sorts of contracting jobs, brokerages, commission agencies, etc., would have been available during periods of relative boom. In short, the Pakistani middle class could be of a nature and size that might not have been fully fathomed.

To go by the general tenor, Pakistani mediapersons seem to be referring to educated, articulate professionals with income sufficient for a comfortable mode of life when they write or speak about the middle class. In other words, they seem to be talking about people like themselves. That section must certainly have grown as there has been a great increase in these types of professions since the start of the IT/Second Industrial Revolution. But that growth has surely been more than matched by the expansion of the segment with roots in the peasantry which now follows newer occupations. Incidentally, the emergence of this peasant-turned-entrepreneur class might account for the demographic shift whereby urban dwellers are said to make up forty per cent of the country's population instead of the twenty per cent of thirty–forty years ago. While this segment is probably less educated than the middle class 'properly so called', it could eventually be more politically significant.

Let us proceed on the assumption that the emergence as a viable political force of the segment made of educated, articulate professionals is what is being spoken about. People making this argument tend to include the vast numbers of retired military personnel within these ranks these days, whereas the *faujis* were earlier considered a different genus if not species. The objective of the inclusion could be to show that the class as a whole has more heft than might be otherwise assumed. It also makes for a feel-good factor all round because of the implicit suggestion that entry into this charmed circle is governed by merit, not inheritance. Such a change—especially in the self-perception of the retirees—is meaningful. More so when it comes with the further assertion that change in class identity coincides with an alteration in the recruitment area of the officer corps.

In a couple of recent interviews that appeared on YouTube, Shuja Nawaz, one of the foremost scholars on the Pakistan Army and brother of former chief Asif Nawaz Janjua, pointed out that in recent years the largest number of inductees into the Military Academy at Kakul came from Karachi, not Jhelum district. While the southern metropolis would have been cited as hometown on application forms, it is impossible to believe that Mohajirs or Sindhis have pipped the people of Punjab and Khyber Pakhtunkhwa in providing sons to the military. What is far more likely is that most of the applicants are the offspring of retired military men from the Potohar and adjoining areas who have settled in Karachi. Similarly, southern Punjab districts are said to be now providing more of the 'Other Ranks' than the three northern revenue divisions. Have Seraikis—hardly considered as equal on the 'martial scale'—actually displaced the boys from the north? Or are these recruits also the sons of men from Pindi and Gujranwala divisions who were settled post-retirement in the canal colonies of the south?

As has been argued in an earlier chapter, the ethos of the 'martial zone' seems to have been preserved but also tweaked by the military as an institution. That being so, the ex-servicemen could be expected to have outlooks quite different from other members of the middle class, say bank officials or lawyers. At the same time, they might carry a special heft because of their institution's history, their discipline and habit of collective functioning. To go by logic and reports about their attitudes, it appears that these retirees see a prominent role for themselves in upholding values or at least striking postures to this effect. From the manner in which the military has constantly portrayed politicians as corrupt, it could be presumed that these *faujis* are even more suffused with the bourgeois sense of righteousness than the rest.

Two other major changes that have taken place since I left Pakistan are the emergence of the young as the major proportion of the population and the phenomenal growth of the media in all its forms. According to official estimates, over 60 per cent of the population is below thirty. The country has an abysmal record in providing education in both private and public sectors and does not seem ready to make much of this demographic dividend. Fears that frustration could drive the youth towards extremist ideologies have been contained for now but few would venture to bet that the battle has been won. Whoever is in power for the next decade and more will have to figure out how to deal with masses of youth with poor education and job prospects.

The terrible consequences of giving free rein to exponents

of extremist ideologies are still fresh in the memory of Pakistani officialdom. We in India cannot really believe that those who let out the *jihadi jinn* have grown to regret it. They do really seem to have. Not out of remorse at what was done to us but out of horror at what the jihadis did to them. Our desire to see them pay for their sins should not blind us to the fact that they did suffer both in terms of deaths in random mass killings as well as the deeply deleterious effect on their economy as a whole. Official Pakistan has learnt the hard way that it will become a target of extremists it creates and that there is no pussyfooting around this problem.

There is enough material floating around to fill idle minds. Circa 1993, Pakistan TV's public affairs programmes were nothing less than cringe inducing. Doordarshan's agro-development programmes were more watchable than PTV's panel discussions and quizzes. Today, their private channels serve up more attention-grabbing fare than the shouting matches that play out in our 'Godi media'. Some of the channel output is often near the top end and some vloggers provide even better fare. Although, as elsewhere, the professional media struggles to sieve out content that is ill-informed, misinformed and uninformed, troll armies are reputedly even more savage than they are in India and what messages are actually striking home is anyone's guess.

All these transformations seem to have coalesced around the middle of the 2010s to create conditions favourable to Imran Khan. After the end of the Musharraf dictatorship, the military-dominated establishment reverted to the system it had operated throughout the 1990s. Under this 'hybrid' form of governance, the establishment retained control over matters of strategic importance—defence, foreign policy, the most vital aspects of the economy—while allowing elected governments to look after development works and public welfare. This system was intrinsically unworkable since there would always be tussles between the military and civilians over issues that fell within both spheres of the hybrid system. For instance, opening of trade with India would make imports cheaper, drain less foreign exchange and provide relief to the people but would also undermine the posture of hostility that the army needed for its own ends. Development works might require foreign aid but the decision to approach donors would not be left to the cabinet alone.

Perhaps the generals initially calculated that civilian cabinets would ultimately buckle. Neither the Pakistan Peoples Party government between 2008 and 2013 nor the Pakistan Muslim League government from 2013 to 2018 turned out to be easy pushovers. In both phases, the military appears to have fallen back on its old ploy of drumming up a media storm against corrupt politicians. Such campaigns pre-empt questions about the system's viability and are designed to make people believe that all would be well once a 'clean' politician is put in place. It is no one's case that Pakistani politicians are 'washed in milk', to use an expression favoured on both sides of the border. However, when the structures for party funding are non-existent, campaigns cost a packet and even the sincerest of representatives has to make provisions for re-election, voters are ready to make some concessions. People turn virulently against politicians when the levels of corruption reach unconscionable levels and/or power is used solely for pelf. A drastic shift in voters' choice can also occur when a leader is able to convince a significant section of the electorate that he is a messiah who will usher in a clean break from the past.

By 2018, the military apparently concluded that in Imran Khan it had found a politician who could be marketed as a change-maker. He had massive name recognition as the captain of the team that won the 1992 Cricket World Cup. Both the *niazi* (paternal) and *burkhi* (maternal) wings of his family were well known for being solidly entrenched in the upper middle class of Lahore even though not in the top rungs of the elite. So what if he had been called 'Im the Dim' during his Oxford days, he had still studied there! The man was surely above corruption since he could ad nauseam repeat the phrase: 'A man like me to whom Allah has given everything can only be in politics for the public good.' His humble attribution of success to the Almighty could not obscure the fact that he, like the officer class of the military, belonged to the meritocracy.

No efforts were apparently spared to ensure that Imran's Pakistan Tehreek-e-Insaf won the 2018 election. Politicians with independent bases—'electables' in the jargon—were persuaded to switch from other parties to the PTI. When that proved insufficient to provide Imran a majority, smaller parties were pushed to support him in parliament. For the next few years, Army Chief Gen Qamar Javed Bajwa and cohorts seemed to take great pride in saying that they and the civilian cabinet were on the same page. They stuck to this line even after it became apparent to every honest and astute observer that matters were going rapidly downhill.

It is mind-boggling that the generals took so long to catch on. From the moment of his great triumph in 1992, it was evident that Imran was incapable of seeking the good of anyone other than himself. With all his countrymen tuned in to his victory speech, the man did not have a word of thanks for their prayers; nor of appreciation for the support staff; nor of acknowledgement for the work—often heroic—of his teammates. It was all about how the victory would help him raise funds for his personal project of building a hospital in his mother's name. After his entry into politics, he would prove that he did not stand for any outlook, any policy or any principles. A man who was expected to bring fresh thinking had no qualms about lauding the most barbarous programmes of the Taliban.

Imran's choices in personnel and policies after becoming premier were just as disastrous. Idealists who had joined his camp were driven out and replaced by some of the most foul-mouthed opportunists to be found in the country. Heads of countries that consistently provided succour to Pakistan—Saudi Arabia and the United Arab Emirates—were insulted; the People's Republic of China, which has invested heavily in major projects, was made to watch helplessly as works floundered; and the United States, which still provides them cutting-edge weaponry was accused of hostility towards him in person. Prolonged negotiations with the International Monetary Fund had produced a bail-out package for the foreign-exchange-strapped economy, only for the Imran government to flout its stipulations in the course of a political struggle. His family and entourage seemed as incapable of keeping its hands off the public wealth as any that had exercised power before.

All the mischief that the army had let loose on the country was finally catching up with it. For the first time since the defeat in the '71 war, the masses were turning against the men in uniform. They were openly abusing the generals for backing a government that was causing them so much harm. It began to dawn on the military that the hybrid system could not be repaired and Bajwa began touting the thesis that 'democracy was the way forward'. The army's decision to withdraw from politics and stay away apparently was backed by most members of the collegium of four and three stars—formation heads and principal staff officers—that is, the Corps Commanders Conference. Once the army switched to this new posture of neutrality, the opposition rallied its members in the National Assembly, persuaded smaller parties and a few members to move across to its side and successfully moved a no-confidence vote. A new coalition government under Shehbaz Sharif, with the PML and PPP at its core, took over in April 2022. But that was not the end of the Imran drama.

It came as no surprise that Imran, inveigling against the military's new-found love for political neutrality, should demand that the generals dismiss the government which had the confidence of the National Assembly, reinstate him in office or at least let him have the main say in the formation of a caretaker government which would oversee fresh elections. What was astounding was that a large proportion of the educated, articulate middle class responded to his call to agitate against his ouster and in support of his demands. Many of those who took to the streets were apparently what are called '*youthias*' (a portmanteau of the English word for the young and a well-known Hindustani expression for the foolish). Older people, who should have known better, made caricatures of themselves by calling for the army to stay involved in politics just when it was finally leaving. A goodly section of ex-servicemen of all ranks were among the agitators. Retired officers were said to have put so much pressure on serving generals that pensions of some had to be suspended in order to bring the rest into line.

Uncertainty prevailed for over half a year and the blame for this rests mainly with Bajwa, according to reports. Although he had let it be known, through his juniors, that he was not interested in a second three-year extension to his tenure in office, he was said to have been manoeuvring for something akin. He was apparently trying to put together a deal whereby he would get a six-month extension during which he would oversee fresh election. His objective apparently was to salvage his reputation.

With Bajwa throwing out signals that he could jump to Imran's side or the other way, there was enormous pressure on the Shehbaz Sharif cabinet to dissolve parliament and call for fresh elections. If the cabinet had succumbed, the consequences could have been disastrous for the Muslim League. The government has earned much opprobrium for the harsh measures taken to stabilize the economy. While the PPP with its feudal base might have won enough seats in Sindh to remain viable, the League could have faced a near wipe-out in Punjab if elections were held before mid-2023. The entire League component of the cabinet went off to London to consult their doughty chief. 'Stay put,' Nawaz Sharif is reported to have told his party people. 'If they (the army) want to throw you out, let them do it. There is no need to oblige them.'

This particular political drama came to a close with the departure of Bajwa from the General Headquarters on 29 November 2022. More accurately, a few days earlier, when the seniormost lieutenant general Asim Munir was promoted to four-star rank and designated the next chief. The army's top leadership was thereby set in proper order and the rest of the institution smoothly settled down. More importantly, it ended Imran's hopes of forcing through an early election by either shaming the army into doing the needful through a barrage of troll attacks or alarming it into doing as much through street agitations.

Imran's Long March for Justice attracted a lot of media attention but it merely meandered through Punjab for weeks before fizzling out around the time Munir became chief. By then, the demagogue's crowd-pulling ability also seemed to have waned despite a small sympathy bump occasioned by a mystifying gun attack on him at a rally. Trolls too had become powerless since the new chief could not be shamed as he had not been involved in the intrigues.

In their assessments of these developments, astute observers seem to take a consensual view that Munir would work at implementing the army's new doctrine of operating within the parameters set for it by the Constitution and the law. Such an assessment is made mainly on the basis of his reputation as an austere professional since he has never made any public pronouncements to this effect. These observers also tend to believe that the doctrine would remain in effect for quite a while as the entire collegium has signed on to it. They point out that circumstances are also not likely to leave Munir with the time or mental bandwidth for political games.

On the other hand, the dynamics of the military as an institution could build pressure for another intervention in politics. After all, the army considers itself the ultimate guardian of the national interest. Since every and all kinds of issues can be brought under the rubric of this term, some future development that a civilian cabinet finds difficult to resolve could provide justification or excuse for the military to intervene.

But, for now, it might not be the India question that grabs Munir's attention. Since India has largely operated in reactive mode and since common sense suggests even more strongly than times before that Pakistan refrain from mischief, there is cause for hope that the ceasefire along the LOC would endure. It would indeed require an unbelievable level of stupidity on Rawalpindi's part to stoke anti-India fires at a time when the situation along Pakistan's western borders was critical.

A day or two after Munir took over, the Tehrik-e-Taliban-e-Pakistan withdrew its ceasefire and followed up almost immediately with armed attacks on security forces. As the TTP and the regime in Kabul are ideologically affiliate, the handling of this challenge would continue to require a fine balancing of counter-insurgency, diplomatic and political measures. While handling the rebels in the border areas, the army would need to find ways of eschewing the sort of actions that had in the past provoked backlash in the interior. As part of the effort to keep the populace in a supportive mood, the army might have to find ways of addressing the disquiet caused by the ripping away of the veil covering the emoluments given to senior officers.

For years, the army has been following a system of rewarding officers with real estate carved out of land acquired for institutional purposes. This has been a legal, if morally dubious, process adopted to offset the perception that salaries and perks were too low. Around the time of Bajwa's retirement a journalistic investigation revealed that the outgoing chief had been granted so much property that his family had attained the status of multi-billionaires. After Munir took over, ordinary Pakistanis began to look up to him, with his iconic status as a straight arrow, to do something about this system of rewards.

With these two major tasks on his agenda, Munir might consider himself lucky for the two seasoned leaders on the other side who can help steer military–civilian relations to a new plane. Whatever their other faults may be, Asif Zardari and Nawaz Sharif—unquestioned leaders of their respective parties—know the necessity of keeping the army out of politics and also the ways of doing so. After all, both have learnt their lessons the hard way and have suffered foisted cases, jail terms, exile in the one case and the assassination of a spouse on the other.

Will the Imran phenomenon turn out to be a passing one? Several corruption cases are already in various stages of investigation and convictions in any of them could lead to disbarment from politics. That need not spell the end of his career since other politicians have bounced back after serving such sentences fully or partially. No political party in Pakistan seems to have a robust organizational structure but the PTI seems to lack even the politician-to-politician networks that the major parties have. It all appears to be very dependent on Imran's personality cult and that might have taken a battering after all the revelations about him and the U-turns he has made. The articulate middle class, which provided much of his support, can be a fickle beast especially when the man they have followed reveals that there is no ballast in his politics.

On the other hand, the two major parties, especially the PML(N), draw support from people who are entrenched in the political process. Their forte is retail politics in which party men act as interfaces between the masses and the officialdom—the local power-brokers to whom ordinary folk turn when they need help with *patwaris, thanedars* and *court sheristadars*. Unlike articulate sections of the populace, such characters are always present, working behind the scenes, and they value leaders who keep their word. These networks were dormant while the youthias were holding forth on the streets but they are probably the repositories of electoral clout at the grassroots.

If this assessment proves accurate, electoral politics could once again become the preserve of the parties that have been around for thirty years and more. These parties have undergone changes in appearance mainly because the younger generation in these dynasty-oriented formations have become active. However, the change appears more than superficial. In interviews and reports about their political moves, Nawaz Sharif and Asif Ali Zardari come across as being far more conscious of the myriad nuances of their polity, more patient and tough-minded than they were before. Each in his own way seems to have realized that stabilizing and making a democratic system workable will be a long-term enterprise and seem ready for it.

Zardari and Sharif have been working together to widen the scope for party-based democracy. They seem to have recognized that while the establishment is not going anywhere it might at last be willing to leave matters largely in the hands of elected politicians. Neither man is a social revolutionary and both seem to believe in plutocrat-led growth. That makes both of them centre-right politicians. However, Zardari never subscribed to the ideological fantasies that gripped Pakistan till nearly the turn of the millennium and Sharif, who paid at least lip service to the Zia-inspired wisdom at the start of his career, discarded it a quarter century ago.

It is appropriate to make a personal confession at this juncture. In like manner as most Indians, I had been taken in by the Benazir delusion before I went to Pakistan. After watching the PPP leader in action, I gradually got put off by her sense of entitlement, her refusal to get serious about matters beyond her own political rewards, her tolerance of corruption and by her lack of commitment to important items on her professed agenda. Still, for as long as I was there and for some time after, I thought that she was preferable to a Muslim League that had been rejuvenated and nourished by Zia-ul-Haq.

My assessment ought to have changed when Nawaz Sharif took on Ishaq Khan. In this I should have taken the cue from Jaffri and Rizvi who recognized the rebellion for what it was even though they could not entirely set aside the misgivings aroused by Sharif's background.

There were other clues that I missed such as the import of Sharif's partnership with Jam Sadiq Ali, chief minister of Sindh from mid-1990 until his death in 1992. At the time, this tie up was seen purely as a method for breaking the PPP in one of its strongest bases and keeping the MQM on a leash. Jam Saab went about both tasks with swagger and a puckish sense of humour.

The story goes that Nusrat Bhutto came face to face with the Jam in the National Assembly soon after his defection. (Sadiq Ali had been a loyal lieutenant of Zulfiqar Ali Bhutto and a prominent figure in PPP politics after his mentor's demise.) Mrs Bhutto scorched the traitor with her eyes and audibly muttered, 'Bastard.'

'Thank you, Mother!' the Jam was said to have replied.

Mohan Narayan, who was the Press Trust of India correspondent in Islamabad from before the start of my tenure to midway through it, once attended a Jam Sadiq Ali press conference in Karachi. He later told me about the manner in which waiters carrying trays filled with glasses of beer did their rounds. As they stopped in front of each guest, the waiters would look at the Jam Saab who would gesture at them to either move on or offer. Mohan thought that drinks were declined to not only those who disliked alcohol but also to those Sadiq Ali did not favour.

In hindsight, it would appear that Sharif from inception was building a coalition of toughened politicians who would stand up to the establishment and his strategy did pay off. Almost all of them stood by him when he took on Ishaq Khan, got thrown out of office, took the matter to court, won his case and was reinstated. Their deeply-felt satisfaction was conveyed to me by Majid Malik who had retired from the army as a lieutenant general but had almost completely transformed himself into a political boss from Chakwal when this conversation took place.

'In the Academy we were taught that we must be defiant in defeat and magnanimous in victory,' Malik said in response to my question about what they proposed to do with Ishaq Khan. They would do nothing, he asserted, though the accompanying smile communicated the unmistakeable message that they thought the defeated president had been left with very little choice.

In that first incarnation as prime minister, Sharif did little to indicate that he would deviate from the establishment's line on important national issues, including by way of giving up his role as a bigger hawk on India than Benazir. However, he did extend to me an unexpected and quite wonderful gesture of kindness. Foreign correspondents in Pakistan briefly formed an association and to launch it decided to invite the Prime Minister for a meal. True Pakistani as he is, Sharif was having none of that. He and no other would be the host, he declared.

So we all assembled at this magnificent hall in the Pindi cantonment. It was pure Raj stuff with a few adjustments. Beautifully maintained building and grounds, tableware and linen of exquisite quality and wine glasses from another time. Those glasses with huge bulbs on long stems had the faint smoky tint that no amount of scrubbing can truly erase but were filled with white and red sherbet. For some reason that I do not recollect now, I was the only Indian in the association. Soup over, everyone was waiting for the *kababs* without which no Pakistani meal could commence and surprised murmurs broke out when the main course was brought on instead. An explanation was soon passed down from chair to chair.

'With the Hindu around we did not think it appropriate to serve beef,' was the reason. It was a bighearted courtesy that had been extended to a journalist who had not been friendly.

Sharif could not cash in on his rebellion because Benazir became prime minister in the 1993 election. But the signs of a readiness to break with the past were very evident when he came close to removing Musharraf from the Chief of Army Staff chair in 1999. This trait was also on display when he served as leader of the opposition in two phases (1993 to 1996 and again from 2008 to 2013). Unlike other opposition leaders, including Benazir to her eternal disgrace, Sharif refrained from openly courting the military or egging it on to remove the elected government. From what I could follow of Pakistani politics from a distance, Sharif apparently went even further in 2013, openly campaigning on an agenda of normalizing relations with India. This amounted to a referendum on not just the military's India policy but on the broader ideological edifice built on it—and he won.

My encounters with Zardari were very few and very brief. On a couple of occasions I almost broke into a trot as I tried to chase the stocky figure with a spring in its walk down a corridor to one of the lifts in the parliament building. Zardari was an under-trial prisoner those days, facing prosecution in a number of corruption cases. (Although he had been given the sobriquet 'Mr Ten Percent', allegedly for the commission he charged for deals made when his wife was prime minister, his defenders always insisted that these were fabricated cases. Zardari's party returned to power in 1993; moved over to the opposition benches in 1996; formed the government again in 2008; and went back to the opposition in 2013. These cases appear to have faded into obscurity over this period.) Between 1990 and '96, he was given parole to attend parliament sessions and those short walks provided the only opportunities for a chat.

On each occasion I managed to get to him as the elevator doors were closing but was unable to get in. A combative grin that had '*harami*' written all over it and a cheery 'Welcome to Pakistan' were all I got for my pains. At that time, he was a youngish man still trying to mark out a political role distinct from his wife's. Today, he is considered a master of the art of stitching coalitions together and of getting the establishment around to his point of view.

Without question, the topmost priority of the PML-PPP government has to be the stabilization of the economy. Pakistan cannot hope to recover from its current economic distress without external financial aid. Unless the International Monetary Fund restarts its assistance programme and donor nations follow its lead, a Sri Lanka type crisis might be unavoidable. A deal could come through but the IMF might not follow through if there is another round of political instability. Cabinet and establishment have stakes in ensuring that the current arrangement stay in place until the flow of aid starts, the economy shows signs of health and benefits begin trickling down to the people.

Consolidation of power by a democratic dispensation would do a world of good for Pakistan. It could also be very beneficial to India. On the last two or three occasions on which it has faced the electorate, the League has openly called for negotiations with India. After taking over as prime minister in 2022, Shehbaz Sharif pointed out that ordinary Pakistanis would be able to buy many commodities at reduced prices if restrictions on trade with India were relaxed. These are not empty slogans since many of the League's oligarchs run businesses or agro-enterprises or represent others who do. They know the value of access to the huge Indian market, more so because of the open secret that the clandestine bilateral trade is many fold larger than what is officially admitted.

A more or less open overture was made by Shehbaz Sharif in an interview to the Dubai-based Al Arabiya channel aired in January 2023. He was guarded in the telecast and his office was quick to put out word that there was no change in the policy as regards Kashmir; that Article 370 must be restored and UN Resolutions must be implemented. However, there were novel formulations such as the one that Pakistan had learned the lessons of three wars and did not want to waste scarce resources on weaponry. While it remains unclear whether this initiative will go anywhere, it certainly would not have been taken without consulting Rawalpindi.

An obvious question that will be raised at this juncture would be about the League's failure in the past to act on its declared intent to enter into negotiations with India. To the equally obvious answer that it was on account of the military's opposition, there would arise the follow up question as to why matters will be any different in future. An answer is that the military too seems to be changing. Rawalpindi seems to have taken in the lesson that everything else depends on a stable economy. Strategists are talking of the need to 'move from geo-politics to geo-economics'—i.e. let the economic interests of the country define its national goals. Clear-headedness would dictate that this is impossible without a healthy relationship with India. (For instance, oil and gas pipelines from West or Central Asia would not be viable unless they traverse Pakistan to touch Indian territory.) But any assessment about the military's change in attitude will need to be repeatedly tested before its veracity is affirmed.

One sign of a change could lie in the fact that the ceasefire along the Line of Control was not violated over two summers. Bajwa delivered on the promise to this effect made at the beginning of 2021. Another sign was that the Pakistan Army chief gave the nod to the opening of talks with India at the time of the political change in April 2022. There are objective conditions shaping this change and those factors are unlikely to vanish.

At present, Pakistan is close to being in the dog house internationally. Imran managed to spoil relations with the US, Saudi Arabia and the United Arab Emirates in the months before his ouster. Even when repairs are made, the situation will not revert to what it was before. India's economic development since 1990 has finally produced the result, which has been logical all along, that the US and other countries have ceased treating Pakistan on par with India.

Although the Taliban took control over the whole of Afghanistan in 2021, the clerics in Kabul are not taking instructions from anyone. Pakistan's past is catching up with it and from now on it will have to ensure that it does not fall foul of the Financial Action Task Force, which has only recently removed the government from the watch list of entities funding terrorism. An end may be in sight to the forty-year policy of bleeding India on the cheap.

At the time I was in Pakistan, the policy of inflicting a myriad cuts on India was gathering momentum. While K.P.S. Gill's policemen were winning the struggle in our Punjab, that fact had either not become clear to the uniforms in Rawalpindi or was ignored in the exhilaration of the early successes in Kashmir. The pursuit of this policy could have also been fuelled by the confidence that India could never find Pakistani social groups that could be used to mount a counter campaign since the minorities were too small in number and sub-nationalist movements had been curbed.

Only later, when Islamist extremists started showing that they could not be controlled and would target military men and civilians in their own country did the Pakistan establishment learn the nature of the monster it had created. It might have come to awareness earlier if it had studied the lessons being thrown up by the war against the communist regime in Afghanistan.

A few months after I took up my assignment, explosions ripped through an arms depot in Nowshera. Initial reports raised fears of a repeat of the Ojhri camp blasts of April 1988 when an estimated 10,000 tonnes of missiles and shells were fired off. Those munitions landed at random in various parts of Islamabad and Rawalpindi killing around a hundred and wounding thousands according to official estimates. The Nowshera blast caused far less damage and I, edging close to the limits of my visa stipulations, made a foray into the civilian parts of the town.

It was in an office of the district administration, with its windows blown off and a crater in the floor, that I came across a clerk salvaging what he could from the wreckage. As soon as he started speaking, I recognized him to be a Pakhtun, so felt emboldened to press my question. What did he think about all this?

'Un logon par bomb phekenge toh woh kya karenge? Wapas guldasta toh nahi phekenge!' (What will they do if you keep throwing bombs at them? Will they throw bouquets back at us?)

He had at the same time bought the official narrative that it was engineered by the Kabul regime and reversed it into an accusation against his own government. Although a part of the official machinery, he as a Pakhtun saw no reason to defend the Punjabi-dominated establishment when it was aiding terror attacks on his own people. Over time the whole Afghan misadventure was to culminate in the formation of the Tehrik-e-Taliban-e-Pakistan that waged an insurgency in Swat and Waziristan, causing the deaths of thousands of soldiers and civilians.

India's success in building an effective counter-insurgency system in Kashmir probably has more than a little to do with the dip in terrorist activity. Over the years, probably after some trial and error, we now have a strong fence along the entire LOC; wide nets cast by central paramilitary forces to cover the towns and the roads connecting them; a gridwork manned by the crack Rashtriya Rifles units to gather intelligence and undertake actions against terror cells; and the hunter-killer packs of the Special Forces battalions of the Parachute Regiment take care of whatever spills through the rest of the system.

With prospects for victory in the Afghan and Kashmir jihads dimming, the Pakistani military appears to have been forced to curb its wilder ambitions. The current economic crisis has caused mutterings about the bloated defence budget. A comment heard recently on a Pakistani discussion site was telling: 'If Bangladesh, which is surrounded by India on three sides, does not feel threatened, why do we?' Freedom from government oversight for the Fauji, Shaheen and Bahriya foundations is being commented upon as is the expansion of Defence Housing Societies.

According to a joke heard recently, a Pakistani diplomat visiting some city in India was called over for drink by a Sikh gentleman sitting in the grounds of the hotel. The Pakistani declined the drink but settled for a chat. His companion started off by observing that Partition had been a mistake.

'Oh, no', thought the foreigner, 'I am going to get another lecture on how we are basically the same people and all that nonsense.'

However, the conversation took an unexpected turn.

'If there had been no Partition,' said the wistful Indian, 'we Punjabis could have imposed military rule all over India. We could've built Defence Housing Societies in every town and each of us could have got a corner plot.'

As the joke indicates, the Pakistan military's penchant

for stuffing itself is inviting open sarcasm. At a more serious level, it has used and betrayed every single political formation and is no longer trusted by the leaders or following of any party. Indoctrination is no longer as effective as it once was in the age of the Internet and propaganda alone cannot stem an institution's alienation from its people. It is not merely goodness of heart that induced Gen Bajwa to re-orient the military towards accepting the narrower parameters set for it by the Constitution.

A mass swing away from the military's influence will perhaps become stronger as the media expands and becomes more liberal. From what we see even in cricket commentating circles, the ripples have started. Wasim Akram, Waqar Younis and Ramiz Raja never seem to have believed in reserving their encouragement and support for players from Pakistan. As inheritor and advancer of the W's pace bowling legacy, Shoaib Akhtar apparently has no qualms about promoting subcontinental harmony. A Pindi native going on TV to declare that Bengalis are the finest race in South Asia is in Pakistan's context nothing less than a revolutionary utterance.

If and when negotiations between India and Pakistan resume, the starting point is likely to be clear enough. Disputes over the Tulbul Navigation Project/Wullar Barrage and Sir Creek are of a socio-economic nature without much emotional overload and could be amenable to early settlement. According to various reports, a deal on the Siachen Glacier was within reach if agreement could be struck on the issue of verifying withdrawals. Perhaps the advances in satellites and remote sensing technology can help push the talks forward. Whether the two-year stand-off between Indian and China in Ladakh will affect talks on the Glacier is not clear.

Musharraf, in an interview given after he left the country, had claimed that he and Manmohan Singh were close to an agreement on Kashmir. From what he said, the contours of this pact were on the lines spoken of in Track Two discussions with a full and final settlement set aside for several decades but interaction across the LOC considerably liberalized. Pakistan's former dictator is not the most reliable of sources and these sorts of proposals have been made so often that reconciliation efforts are unlikely to gain credence until the document is close to signing.

A resolution of these outstanding issues might not of itself usher in an era of great bonhomie. Are we in India likely to forget in a hurry the numerous atrocities that Pakistan has engineered against our people? Or the intense, relentless, communally-charged hostility that has been fostered and unleashed against us? Our children might be taught about the wars that we have fought but they have not been instructed to look at the people of neighbouring countries as objects of hate. All this has been done against us by Pakistan and our people are unlikely to forgive or forget until they are convinced that there have been fundamental changes in respect of such matters across the border.

For a fundamental change to occur, the whole edifice of indoctrination has to be dismantled first of all. Pakistanis need to learn that the horrors of Partition were not committed solely by Hindus and Sikhs. They need to know that the UNSC resolutions on Kashmir stipulated that Pakistan had to withdraw its troops from all of the State as it was in August 1947 before further measures can be taken. They have to understand that the creation of Bangladesh in 1971 was on account of the racist stupidity of their leaders and not contrived by Indian perfidy. Forget about South Asian peace and friendship. Pakistanis need to dump this whole ideological baggage and stop their military from moulding their minds in this way, just so that they can live normally.

We too need to address a few fundamental facts. Not for the sake of Pakistan or friendly relations between the two countries but for own mental balance. First off, the far right dream of an Akhand Bharat and the liberal dream of reducing Partition to irrelevance are just that—fantasies. Pakistan is a separate part of the sub-continent like Nepal, Bhutan, or Bangladesh and it will remain as such. Even if South Asia becomes a common market some day in the distant future, our separate histories and the cultures born of those will make us distinct from one another and the sooner we learn this truth the better.

Akhand Bharat must be among the most absurd concepts thrown up by political thought since its achievement will nullify the ultimate objective desired by those who advocate it. To go by the 2011 census figures, Muslims made for 17.2 crores in a total population of 130 crores. Pakistan's population is estimated to be 22.09 crores of which only a very small proportion are minorities. Bangladesh has 16.47 crore people of which less than 10 per cent are non-Muslims. If all these populations were to be merged into one polity, the Muslim block would form 56 plus crores of a total 180 crores. Non-Muslim numbers in the new entity would at best have grown by about 2 or 3 crores. From dealing with 13.5 per cent or so of Muslims in present-day India, Hindus of this Akhand Bharat would have to deal with 31 per cent.

When Akhand Bharat is a Hindu-majoritarian project, as it surely is, how do these numbers make any kind of sense? If the idea is that all of South Asia will become a Hindu land with no non-Hindu people, how is that going to be achieved? Through mass conversions? It has taken 800 years since the start of the Delhi Sultanate to move such a chunk of people one way. How long will it take to move them the other? Even if we could summon the moral depravity to commit genocide or ethnic cleansing on a truly gigantic scale, are nearly half a billion people going to accept such a fate meekly? Will the rest of the world let us?

In a way, the liberal dream of a South Asia sans borders is the other side of the Akhand Bharat coin. It is not going to happen because majorities in the other countries do not want it. They have got used to their own systems. Besides, when we have not socialized all our people into a truly liberal, secular society after 75 years of trying, how are we going to accommodate anther 400 million or so people who have spent most of that time under the influence of dictators and clerics.

Certain steps that could be taken in the short term make sense. Our present government will probably insist that its policy of 'no talks till terrorism is ended' has worked. It could be argued that the signs of Pakistani de-escalation could be attributable to other factors as well.

Without getting deeper into that I would suggest that the history of sanctions all over the world shows that these measures hurt people of goodwill—those interested in working for amity—as much if not more than the ill-intentioned.

To apply pure logic, would we not create constituencies for amity inside Pakistan if we were a bit more generous in allowing deserving people there to come to India for medical treatment or higher education? Will not the creation of such constituencies help us? For that our policy for granting visas needs to be sharply focused. Two episodes can be provided as illustrations.

Before boarding the PIA flight for the first time, I walked into the duty free shop in Palam (I do not think it was Indira Gandhi International at that time) Airport. The man at the counter asked me where I was going. When I said Lahore he laughed and told me to keep the bottle back on the shelf since Pakistan Customs would not let me take it in. Then I boarded and wondered what the man was talking about.

A few seats in rows front and back of mine were occupied by men shoddily dressed and crudely behaved. As I looked on, each of them loaded paper-covered packages into the overheads bins. Despite the cover, I could make out that each was a parcel of four Scotch whiskey bottles in light cardboard cases. A blatant smuggling racket going on at a time when family visas (i.e. visas for Mohajirs visiting their kin in India) were hard to come by.

Far better results can surely be attained if law-abiding and decent people are allowed to visit. Perhaps families could be let in as part of tour groups to a wide range of destinations. Such an arrangement could help weed out the undesirables and at the same time give peaceable people a chance to see the good parts of India, scenery and character-wise. Instead, the decent are blocked while scum with no stakes in normalization—in fact to the contrary—cross the borders with apparent ease.

The second episode shows the good effect a sensible approach can have. Balakh Sher Mazari, a hefty Sindhi feudal full of bonhomie, was caretaker prime minister in that interlude between Nawaz Sharif's first ouster and his reinstallation by the Supreme Court. Mazari called all five of us Indian correspondents over to his house for a cup of tea. After a long discussion about matters of high import we moved on to lighter topics. Lighter than the five of us had bargained for.

Mazari had been one of the lucky people who was granted a visa to watch the 1982 Asian Games in Delhi. He, family and friends drove across in convoy. As he narrated the story, one could imagine him in Awami and tweed jacket, with perhaps a scarf neatly rolled and tucked in at the throat lolling in a chair at one of the *dhabas* along the highway south of Jalandhar. 'We had a great time during that journey,' he told us on that evening eleven years after the event, 'Good food, good fun, beer, sheer and all that.'

What a fantastically expansive idea of India must have been presented to that group of Pakistanis. Whether it leads to peace or not, that is the way we should be seen by others. As people who live big, even if everyone does not go for beer, sheer and all that.

ALSO FROM SPEAKING TIGER

WHERE THE INDUS IS YOUNG

A Winter in Baltistan

Dervla Murhpy

'Altogether the most appallingly fascinating travel book I have ever read.'—Jan Morris

One winter in the mid-1970s, Dervla Murphy, her six-year-old daughter Rachel and Hallam, a hardy mule, walked into Baltistan close to Pakistan-held Kashmir—the frozen heart of the Western Himalayas. For three months they travelled along the perilous Indus Gorge and into nearby valleys, making a mockery of fear, trekking through the forbidding Karakoram mountains and lodging with the Balts, who farm one of the remotest regions on earth. Despite the hardship, Dervla never forgot the point of travel, retaining enthusiasm for her magnificent surroundings and using her sense of humour to bring out the best in her hosts, who were often locked into the melancholic mood of mid-winter.

This hair-raising, quirky and vivid account of their adventure is a classic of travel writing.